My Sap is Rising

A Pilgrimage of Holistic Mental Health Healing with Hildegard of Bingen and Alfred Adler

Danae Ashley, M.Div., M.A., LMFT

Illustrated by
Kester Limner

Copyright © 2025 by Danae Ashley

All rights reserved.

No part of this book may be reproduced in any form or by any electronic or mechanical means, including information storage and retrieval systems, without written permission from the author, except for the use of brief quotations in a book review.

All images of Hildegard's illuminations are from Rupertsberg Scivias Codex of Saint Hildegard of Bingen, around 1175, original lost since 1945, hand copy on parchment 1930, Abbey of St. Hildegard, Rüdesheim-Eibingen and used with permission.

The author does not consent to this work being used for training artificial intelligence systems.

All photographs are the author's.

Tehom Center Publishing is a 501(c)3 nonprofit publishing feminist and queer authors, with a commitment to elevate BIPOC writers.

Paperback ISBN: 978-1-966655-68-8

Ebook ISBN: 978-1-966655-69-5

Contents

HOW TO USE THIS BOOK	15
Hildegard of Bingen	17
Alfred Adler	18
Your invitation awaits…	20
1. WHAT CREATES A HEALER?	**21**
Family and Social Context	25
Visions and Illnesses	28
The Importance of Place	37
Pilgrim's Reflection	41
Benediction	44
2. HOLISM	**45**
A Gardener's Approach	
Slow Medicine	46
Viriditas	52
What is Viriditas?	54
Pilgrim's Reflection	57
Benediction	60
3. VICES AND VIRTUES	**63**
A Recipe for Healing	
The Soul's Journey	65
Virtues	68
Vices	73
The 'S' Word	74
Seeking Virtues in Core Values	78
Pilgrim's Reflection	81
Benediction	83
4. THE FOUR TEMPERAMENTS OF PERSONALITY	**85**
Who Doesn't Love a Personality Test?	86
The Four Temperaments	90
Choleric	94
Melancholic	96
Phlegmatic	99
Sanguine	102

A Note on Lunar Prognostication	105
Pilgrim's Reflection	108
Benediction	109

5. MEDIEVAL MENTAL HEALTH, AILMENTS, AND CURES — 111
- Mental Health Ailments — 113
- Melancholy — 116
- Anger — 122
- Madness — 127
- Magic and the Devil's Hatred — 133
- Pilgrim's Reflection — 137
- Benediction — 140

6. RITUALS FOR HEALING — 143
- What is Ritual? — 146
- Ritual and Similar Terms: Some Definitions — 147
- Recipes, Miracles, and Exorcism, oh my! — 149
- Pilgrim's Reflection — 160
- Benediction — 162

7. THERE IS NO MENTAL HEALTH WITHOUT COMMUNITY — 165
- Exorcism as a Healing Rite — 166
- Case Study: The Exorcism of Lady Sigewize — 168
- What can we learn from this case study? — 172
- Pilgrim's Reflection — 175
- Benediction — 176

8. EMBODIED CREATIVITY IN HEALING — 183
- Visual Art — 185
- Praying with Hildegard's Illuminations — 188
- Mandalas and Prayer — 189
- The Healing Power of Singing Together — 190
- Relic Collecting — 193
- Drama and Dance — 195
- Pilgrim's Reflection — 198
- Benediction — 202

9. HILDEGARD'S OWN MENTAL HEALTH — 203
- Migraines or Neurodiversity or Something Else? — 204
- Being a Wounded Healer — 206

	Pilgrim's Reflection	211
	Benediction	212
10.	FINAL THOUGHTS	215
	Pilgrim's Reflection	216
	Benediction	217
	Works Cited	219
	Additional Resources	229
	Acknowledgments	235

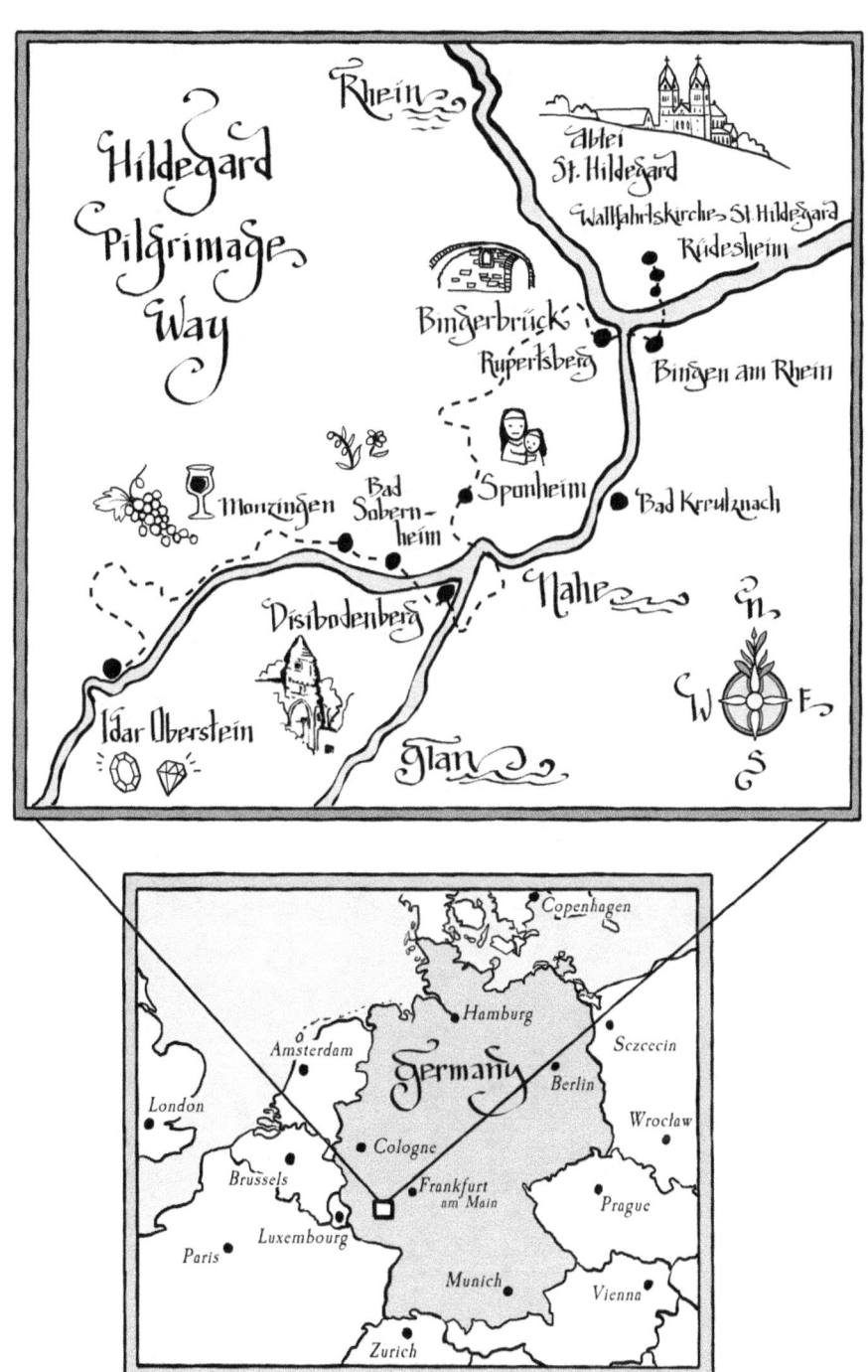

For Dr. Eve Bernstein and all those devoted to caring for women's health—physically, emotionally, and spiritually

Preface

In January 2023, I had been ministering with a church as a part-time Associate Rector for almost five years. We were in clergy transition and had just hired an Interim Rector in December. I had been wounded by the broader Church in multiple ways and felt I was finally healing. At the same time, I was researching a project for my first sabbatical on Hildegard of Bingen and her idea of healing and *viriditas* when the Vestry (church board) decided to balance the budget by eliminating my position. I had stayed with them through the COVID-19 pandemic and planned on staying until they discerned a new rector (senior pastor)—about two years, pursuing God's call outside of congregational ministry a month or two after the new rector arrived. Leaving on my own terms was not to be.

Instead, I was thrown into a wilderness of grief and scrambling to figure out how I would pay my bills and help take care of my family. I was in a fog, yet one thing was clear when I entered prayer: I needed to go to Hildegard in Germany.

I had a conversation with my dear friend and fellow priest, Keely, as this plan crystallized. She had lived in Germany and spoke fluent German, so I asked for help in contacting the Abtei St. Hildegard in Eibingen. Keely did some research and quickly found that there was an English version of a guidebook called *The Hildegard of Bingen Pilgrimage Book*.[1] I ordered it and began to plan for May.

I reached out to the author, Dr. Annette Esser, who had advocated for the pilgrimage way to become an official German trail and asked if we could meet. Dr. Esser was extremely kind in her response, and we set a date to meet toward the end of my journey.

---

1. Esser, Annette. *The Hildegard of Bingen Pilgrimage Book*. Collegeville: Liturgical Press. 2022.

We met in Bingen at the Hildegard Forum, a restaurant, shop, and medicinal herb garden, for an early dinner after a long day of driving to some of my last tableaus—large rectangular signs with images from Hildegard's visions, quotes on the theme, and a reflection question. I had rented a car because I was still recovering from recent foot surgery. A tall woman with a broad smile and stylish, colorful clothes greeted me. We had a wonderful conversation, and at the end, she invited me to dinner the next day at her home in Bad Kreuznach, a spa town about 25 minutes away. It would be my last night in Germany, so I agreed. I was "a feather on the breath of God," as Hildegard would say.

The next evening, I pulled up to a historic building in a charming neighborhood. Annette met me at the door and explained the history of the house—it was a family home, and she lived in the flat on the main floor and ran the Scivias Institute from there while allowing friends of Hildegard who were there to study or visit to stay in the flat above hers.

Instead of having dinner at her flat, Annette took me to downtown Bad Kreuznach because she wanted me to see where they were going to have the next international Hildegard conference in 2024. The theme was *Hildegard von Bingen: Wellness and Healing* and with the Nahe River running through it, vineyards surrounding it, and mineral water baths and misting for health, it was the ideal setting for the conference.

The weather was mild, so we ate outdoors at an Italian restaurant. Talking with Annette was delightful. She is a true visionary with passion for creative projects that reminded me of the energy I imagined our beloved Hildegard would have had. We were talking about the way Hildegard healed people when Annette suggested that I come back and do a presentation about Hildegard and psychotherapy at the September 2024 conference. I was so surprised that I looked behind me to make sure she was talking to me! I explained to her that I had done a cursory look at the topic online and only found a few books exploring archetypes and other

Jungian topics in Hildegard's life and visions,[2] but nothing on her general treatment for mental illness or what we would classify as modern-day psychotherapy.

Annette looked at me intently and proclaimed, "I'll tell you what my advisor, Ann Belford Ulanov [a distinguished Jungian analyst and professor] at Union Theological Seminary told me when I had questions about my thesis: That is because this is your work to do." I sat there stunned by the truth of it. I felt my own *viriditas*—the term Hildegard called the life force, the greening power of God—bubble up like sap rising. A cosmic "Yes" hummed through me. In that moment, Annette was my own Sybil on the Rhine—a prophetess—as Hildegard was once called. By the time I got back to the Hildegard Forum for the night, I already had an outline for the presentation and quickly realized that there was going to be so much information and learning that I would need to write this very book.

Hildegard has a way of connecting you with a vast world beyond what you thought you knew. Through her devotion to God and faithfulness in her work, she has inspired a global community stretching back through the centuries of which I am now a member. Studying her healing methods for mental health and connecting them to our 21st century understanding of psychotherapy has been a true joy and I am delighted to share them with you here.

Danae M. Ashley
Feast Day of St. Hildegard 2025

---

2. I resonate with and respect the Jungian approach to Hildegard and highly recommend Avis Clendenen's 2012 book *Experiencing Hildegard: Jungian Perspectives*.

How To Use This Book

Going on pilgrimage means entering a liminal space, best done at a transitional time in your life—much like deciding to begin psychotherapy. You come to each because something in your life needs to change, often leading deeper and in other directions than what you initially assumed. Both are sojourns within that cannot come to fruition except through the aid of an outside community. The ministry of presence should never be discounted. Other pilgrims on the way, guides, and unexpected helpers are all part of the restoration, witnessing your pain, transformation, and growth. You cannot separate the healing that comes from this witness.

Pilgrimage, like psychotherapy, demands that you leave behind your comfortable ways to become unmoored so that new wayfinders become clear and the destination open. You are not the same as when you started. Your spirit expands for healing as new guideposts draw near. *Who am I without all this?* becomes both the question and answer lived through the journey.

In St. Hildegard of Bingen's fourth vision of her first work, *Scivias*, she calls the Soul a "pilgrim" returning by God's grace after

Danae Ashley, M.Div., M.A., LMFT

being on a path of error.[1] In her morality play, *Ordo Virtutum* (*Order of the Virtues*), the Soul is on a pilgrimage—defending itself against vices and the Devil by way of utilizing virtues and keeping its heart set on God. The idea of the soul on a pilgrimage to return to God from this transitory life is not new. People throughout the centuries have found pilgrimage to be spiritually fulfilling and emotionally healing. As an Episcopal priest and Adlerian-trained marriage and family therapist, I have witnessed this firsthand. Yet I never had the intention of going on pilgrimage myself until faced with my own liminal circumstances in 2023. Pilgrimage became the surprising motivation for this work you now hold.

This book is an invitation to pilgrimage for personal or group discovery and healing. You will journey with me as I revisit parts of my pilgrimage on the Hildegard of Bingen Pilgrimage Way woven together with the works of two people who have been major influences on me and who I have come to love: Hildegard of Bingen and Alfred Adler. Though they lived eight centuries apart, they both approached mental health healing holistically.

Part spiritual memoir, part self-help, and part educational, there is something for everyone in these pages. *A Pilgrim Ponders* are questions for the individual to think on within each chapter to help you go deeper as you read. The *Pilgrim's Reflection* section at the end of each chapter includes questions you can use for individual or group reflection, followed by a Benediction with group options to close the chapter. As we say in the Episcopal Church, "All may, some should, none must," so please engage in what feels right for you.

Many people have never heard of either Adler or Hildegard and some sections may feel more academic in style than others because I want to give useful psychoeducational and spiritual information. Others may know a little (or a lot) about Hildegard or Adler and

---

1. Hildegard of Bingen, Caroline Walker Bynum, and Barbara Newman. *Hildegard of Bingen: Scivias*. Translated by Mother Columba Hart and Jane Bishop. First Edition. New York: Paulist Press, 1990, p. 109.

can bring their knowledge to fill in a fuller context of the bits I have shared here. This work is not exhaustive by any means. My hope is that this information will spur you to do your own deep dive into the topics that interest you most. My footnotes and bibliography will be good resources for your journey.

Two important notes:

- *Language:* Both Hildegard and Adler lived in times when masculine language was used for the universal experience. I keep this language in their direct quotes with awareness that understanding of gendered language in contemporary Western culture is continually evolving. I also use *italics* for block quotes from Hildegard and Adler's work for ease of reading.
- *Disclaimer:* This book and its exercises and ideas are not to take the place of professional therapy, spiritual direction, and/or your physician, nor should you try any of Hildegard's prescriptions at home. If this book brings up tender places in you, please reach out to a professional healthcare provider for support and further guidance.

And now, let me introduce you to your two companions on this way.

Hildegard of Bingen

A remarkable figure in medieval history, Hildegard of Bingen (1098-1179) was a German Benedictine[2] nun, Christian mystic, visionary, healer, preacher, musician, composer, environmentalist, writer, language creator (*lingua ignota*), and advisor to many who

---

2. Benedictines are the name for the Roman Catholic Order of St. Benedict (OSB) founded by Benedict of Nursia in 529 and follow the *Rule of St. Benedict*. They are the oldest of all the religious orders in the Roman Catholic Church.

held secular and spiritual power in medieval Europe. Her medieval holism and interpretation of *viriditas*—the greening spirit—as part of the healing process can be applied to modern day practices in mental health.

While celebrated as a saint in the Roman Catholic Church and other traditions for centuries, she was officially given equivalent canonization on May 10, 2012 and the title of Doctor of the Universal Church on October 7, 2012 by Pope Benedict XVI. She is only the fourth woman to receive that title, joining Catherine of Siena, Teresa of Avila, and Therese of Lisieux—all nuns and mystics. I was present for the celebration of the anniversary of her canonization in 2023 at the Hildegard Parish Church in Rüdesheim am Rhein, where the relics of her tongue and heart reside. It was truly a time of joy for Eibingen Abbey and the wider community.

The bibliography contains many excellent resources for the exploration of Hildegard's background and myriad of gifts. For the scope of this work, I will include limited and relevant information that applies to understanding Hildegard as a healer, along with the threads of modern-day psychotherapy that can be pulled through from her experiences.

Alfred Adler

What could a revolutionary 12th century German Benedictine nun and a 20th century Austrian physician and psychotherapist have to do with one another? I pondered this question as a sojourner on the

Pilgrimage Way, driving through the winding roads of the lush Rhine Valley, Hildegard's homeland, approximately nine hours' drive northwest of Alfred Adler's birthplace of Vienna. The more I learned about Hildegard, the more I connected back to my training as an Adlerian psychotherapist—their holistic approaches to healing were similar despite being centuries apart.

Follow your heart but take your brain with you.

Alfred Adler was born into a Jewish family on February 7, 1870, the second of seven children. Adler suffered various illnesses growing up, which later inspired him to become a physician. He attended the University of Vienna and became an ophthalmologist at first, then went into general practice, finally landing in psychiatry. Both he and Carl Jung were part of Sigmund Freud's circle, Adler going his own way in 1911 and Jung in 1914. Adler went on to develop his Individual Psychology, a holistic approach to psychotherapy, influenced by his training as a doctor. This differed from Jung's focus on the collective unconscious, individuation, and archetypes shaping personality by placing emphasis on social embeddedness, feelings of inferiority (Adler coined the term 'inferiority complex'), and the striving for superiority which influenced personality.

Adler lectured all over the world throughout his professional life and was one of the first in psychology to support feminism. He addressed the myth of masculine superiority and woman's alleged inferiority, arguing that social and cultural norms rather than biology were at the root of gender differences. Adler immigrated to the United States in 1934 and continued his work until his death in 1937 while on a lecture tour in Aberdeen, Scotland.

There are a few Adlerian graduate schools in the U.S., and I attended the Adler Graduate School in the Minneapolis area where

Danae Ashley, M.Div., M.A., LMFT

I focused on marriage and family therapy while becoming distinctly Adlerian in my therapeutic orientation. Adlerians connect through local chapters of the North American Society for Adlerian Psychology (NASAP) and international gatherings such as the International Association of Individual Psychology (IAIP) conference, spreading Adler's legacy far and wide. You can learn more about Adler and his work through the resources listed in the bibliography.

Your invitation awaits...

I invite you to open your heart, mind, and spirit to the pilgrimage through these pages. To inspire you, here is one of my favorite stories found in Hildegard's letter to Odo of Soissons (1148). She writes:

> *Listen: A king sat upon his throne, surrounded by lofty and wonderfully beautiful columns, ornamented with ivory and bearing the banners of the king proudly to all. Then it pleased the king to lift a small feather from the ground, and he commanded it to fly. Yet a feather does not fly because of anything in itself, but because the air bears it along. Thus, I am a feather on the breath of God, not gifted with great powers or education, nor even with good health but I rely completely on God.*[3]

May you be a feather on the breath of God and find your own sap rising as you journey.

---

3. Kujawa-Holbrook, Sheryl A., translator. *Hildegard of Bingen: Essential Writings and Chants of a Christian Mystic—Annotated & Explained*. 1st edition, SkyLight Paths, 2016, 57.

Chapter 1
What Creates a Healer?

It was the quiet I first noticed as I began the uphill walk to the Disibodenberg, the ancient ruin of the monastery where Hildegard of Bingen spent 40 years of her life. It was not silent, but the layered quiet of nature heightened by the absence of sounds from modern living. The air smelled of fecund earth, spring plants unfurling, and the lushness of what was to come. As I walked through the gentle hush, punctuated  by birdsong and the ebb and flow of breeze, I gazed in wonder through the trees and foliage at glimpses of the lichen-covered stones. I was, perhaps, walking somewhere that Hildegard had walked.

Some of the structures looked like they could have been in mid-construction or disintegration depending on which end of the time spectrum you were on. Who knows? It is a magical place, a thin place of the world, where one moves in *Kairos*—time outside of time—instead of *Chronos*—chronological time.

Danae Ashley, M.Div., M.A., LMFT

According to the legend, Disibodenberg was founded by an Irish monk, St. Disibod, who had come from Ireland to then-Francia in 640. He came to rest on a hill at the convergence of the Nahe and Glan rivers. Putting his walking stick in the ground, it began sprouting leaves and a "white doe scratched a freshwater spring into the ground."[1] After Disibod's death, it became a pilgrimage place of miracles, and a church and monastery were founded there. The monastery was destroyed twice by Vikings and then Magyar invaders between 882 and the early 900s CE. It was abandoned until 1100, when Bishop Willigis entrusted it and several surrounding towns and farms to twelve Augustinian canons. In 1107, the monastery was given by Archbishop Ruthard to a group of Benedictines from Mainz where they began construction of a new monastery church. The church was not completed until 1143, so construction was ongoing almost the entire time Hildegard lived there.

I thought of this as I reached the summit of the hill, struck by the vastness of what had clearly taken up the whole of the hilltop to have left such immense ruins. What must it have been like for Hildegard as she came to this place, most likely journeying on foot from Sponheim, where she had been staying with her pious kinswoman, Jutta? Jutta, Hildegard, and another young woman were enclosed as anchorites[2] at the Disibodenberg in a solemn rite on the Feast of All Saints', 1 November 1112.[3] Hildegard was about 14 years old, and Jutta about 20. It may have been cold and possibly overcast or rainy, knowing German weather in November, as the funeral-like prayers were said and the stones were stacked, one by

---

1. Evans, C. P. *Hildegard of Bingen, Two Hagiographies: Vita Sancti Rupperti Confessoris and Vita Sancti Dysibodi Episcopi*. Bilingual edition. Paris: Peeters, 2010.
2. An anchorite is a religious recluse who takes a vow to live in permanent confinement in a cell or room attached to a church or community while living a life of prayer and spiritual service.
3. Silvas, Anna. *Jutta and Hildegard: The Biographical Sources*. 1st edition. University Park, PA: Penn State University Press, 1999, 54.

one, diminishing the light until the door was sealed like a tomb with the living saints[4] inside.

We cannot compare Hildegard's experience of being 14 years old with our contemporary experience of the same age. Biologically, children experienced the onset of puberty at similar ages to today, unless there was a delaying factor such as illness or malnutrition.[5, 6] However, socially and psychologically, there are clear differences. While those in their teens may have been referred to as youths, there was no term of adolescence as we define it today: a lengthy time of discovering one's identity.

In medieval Germany, the distinguishing factors between childhood and adulthood were the biological markers of girls having the onset of menarche and boys growing pubescent hair, and the social markers of menarche signaling being of marriageable age for girls and boys being of age to become knights or apprentice in a trade or other work.[7] Of course, they could also be dedicated to the Church, as Hildegard was. There was simply no time of adolescence as we experience it—they were children and then they were adults, nothing in between. Discerning parents paid close attention to their children's dispositions and would try to align them with vocations that suited them. The children understood their place in the hierarchal world, even when it was difficult. Hildegard had been dedicated to the Church since birth and by the time she was 14, was prepared to begin the life of a Benedictine anchoress.

Before I made my ascent to the Disibodenberg, I stopped by the

---

4. Mulder-Bakker, Anneke B. "Anchorites in the Low Countries." In *Anchoritic Traditions of Medieval Europe*, edited by Liz Herbert McAvoy, 22–42. Boydell & Brewer. https://www.jstor.org/stable/10.7722/j.ctt81hf3.8. 2010, 41.
5. Lewis, Mary. "Children Aren't Starting Puberty Younger, Medieval Skeletons Reveal." The Conversation. February 12, 2018. http://theconversation.com/children-arent-starting-puberty-younger-medieval-skeletons-reveal-91095.
6. Papadimitriou, Anastasios. "The Evolution of the Age at Menarche from Prehistorical to Modern Times." *Journal of Pediatric and Adolescent Gynecology* 29 (6): 527–30. https://doi.org/10.1016/j.jpag.2015.12.002. 2016.
7. Schultz, James A. "Medieval Adolescence: The Claims of History and the Silence of German Narrative." *Speculum* 66 (3): 519–39. https://doi.org/10.2307/2864225. 1991.

entrance to get my pilgrimage stamp[8] and experienced one of a pilgrim's prized bounties: a restroom. When I came out, I noticed there were people in the museum, which had been closed a few minutes earlier. The sign said it was only open on the weekends and by appointment and this was a Tuesday afternoon at 3:00. I felt the movement of the Holy Spirit in this moment and opened the door. There were two women there: one introduced herself as the small museum's curator[9] and the other was a filmmaker from Los Angeles who was researching a film about Hildegard. What a small world! I explained who I was and what I was doing, and the curator took pity on me and told me to take a quick peek at the museum while she finished speaking with the filmmaker.

When she was finished, I asked her some questions and discovered that they think they know where Hildegard and Jutta were enclosed. I was surprised because the ruins were so old and none of Hildegard's writings or writings about Jutta talk about exactly where in the Disibodenberg they lived. She explained that during that period, all Benedictine monasteries were designed to be built the exact same way. It was rare that there was any deviance from the architectural plan, and if there was, it was for a specific reason. Anchorites were not uncommon during the 12th century and would be enclosed at the walls of a monastic church because being close to the monastic community was spiritually

---

8. In this pilgrimage way and others, pilgrims will have small booklets to stamp at different stations throughout their journey.
9. I do not remember this wonderful woman's name, but I do remember she was originally from Italy, spoke some English, and had come there on a bicycle. I am forever indebted to her kindness in letting me tour the museum and answering my questions.

necessary.[10] Although walled in, the women's cell would have had a small window in which they would be able to hear and partake in the liturgies and prayers, as well as pass things out and receive food and other items. The curator told me to find the sign for the Church of the Canons and I would see where Hildegard was most likely enclosed. This was more than I could have hoped.

So, as I walked around the top of the hill, marveling at the extensive monastery Disibodenberg must have been in its heyday, I wandered my way to the sign that had a picture of what looked like a wall built outside of another wall. Taking my smartphone and using my trusty translation app, I breathed in awe as the words revealed that this, indeed, was the Church of the Canons, and attached to it was what translated as "Extension after 1108 for the first women's hermitage." I said a prayer of thanksgiving as I walked reverently into the rectangular space where Hildegard may have spent the first part of her 38 years at Disibodenberg before more women came, attracted to Jutta's leadership, and they outgrew the space. It was not large, maybe the size of an American living room, long and not deep. I closed my eyes as I felt myself respond with emotion to being part of the space and I listened for Hildegard's echo through time.

Family and Social Context

Not much is known about Hildegard's early life. She was born into a noble family in 1098 possibly in the town of Bermersheim near Alzey[11] or the village of Niederhosenbach[12] between Kirn and Idar-

---

10. Signori, Gabriela. "Anchorites in German-Speaking Regions." In *Anchoritic Traditions of Medieval Europe*, edited by Liz Herbert McAvoy, 43–61. Boydell & Brewer, 2010 https://www.jstor.org/stable/10.7722/j.ctt81hf3.9. 58.
11. Maddocks, Fiona. *Hildegard of Bingen: The Woman of Her Age*. Main edition. Faber & Faber, 2013, 9.
12. Esser, Annette. *The Hildegard of Bingen Pilgrimage Book*. Collegeville: Liturgical Press, 2022.

Oberstein. Tradition tells that she was the tenth child[13] of Hildebert of Bermersheim and Mechtild of Merxheim-Nahet. Official records show that there were only seven older siblings: Drutwin, Hugo, Roricus, Irmengard, Odilia, Jutta, and Clementia are mentioned specifically.[14] I wonder, if the ten children were not just a literary device used by Guibert of Gembloux to create a theological allegory to the principle of tithing[15] and strengthen Hildegard's saintly image, perhaps two were lost as either miscarriages or stillbirths.[16] It is noted that Hildegard was a sickly child with, as she says in her autobiographical writing, "a recurring ailment I have suffered from my mother's milk until now, which wore out my flesh and sapped my strength."[17] Infant sickness and mortality in the Middle Ages was high, often because of nutritional depletion,[18] and perinatal loss was common, just as it is today,[19] although rarely talked about or recorded.[20]

Hildegard may or may not have been a formal child oblation to the Church—a common practice in the early medieval period tied

---

13. Flanagan, Sabina. *Hildegard of Bingen: A Visionary Life*. 2nd edition. Hoboken: Routledge, 1998, 23.
14. Ibid., 207
15. Tithing is the Biblical tenant from Leviticus 27:30-32 of giving 10% or a tenth part of one's money and possessions, additionally in contemporary Christianity—time and talent—as a sacrifice to God to support a religious establishment or faith community.
16. There is no direct evidence for this. I offer this alternative idea as a speculation based on my work and research on fertility struggle and perinatal loss.
17. Silvas, Anna, ed. and trans. *Jutta and Hildegard: The Biographical Sources*. University Park, PA: Pennsylvania State University Press, 1999, 158-159
18. Grupe, G. and G. Hühne-Osterloh. "Causes of Infant Mortality in the Middle Ages Revealed by Chemical and Palaeopathological Analyses of Skeletal Remains." *Zeitschrift Für Morphologie Und Anthropologie* 77, no. 3 (1989): 247–58. http://www.jstor.org/stable/25757245.
19. "Why We Need to Talk about Losing a Baby." Accessed November 5, 2024. https://www.who.int/news-room/spotlight/why-we-need-to-talk-about-losing-a-baby.
20. There is a beautiful theological essay in "Chapter Four: Comfort" from the book *Hope Deferred* edited by Nadine Pence Frantz and Mary T. Stimming that uses Martin Luther's pastoral letter, "Comfort for Women Who Have Had a Miscarriage" from 1542 as its basis which may deepen the understanding of perinatal loss on parents in earlier centuries.

to the Rule of St. Benedict for which there was a ritual framework.[21] Regardless, she was dedicated to the Church from birth and did not go to live with her distant kinswoman, Jutta of Sponheim, daughter of Count Stephen of Sponheim, until she was eight years old. Jutta was about six years Hildegard's elder and a devoted Christian who promised God she would dedicate herself to religious life if she survived a terrible illness at age 12.[22] Jutta was Hildegard's mentor until her death in 1136.[23] She was known for her piousness and asceticism, which Hildegard later turned away from in favor of moderation.

From a family systems perspective, if I were to do a genogram or family constellation (a three-generation family map) of Hildegard's family of origin, we would include Jutta as a significant person having influence over her life. From an Adlerian perspective, Mechtild (her mother) and Jutta would be her feminine guiding lines, teaching her what it meant to be a woman of her time. Hildebert (her father) and later Volmar, the monk who became her secretary and confidant, would be her masculine guiding line. Adler believed that a person's lifestyle or personality was fully developed between the ages of five and seven, including a self-concept, idea of the world (called *Weltbild*—an especially important concept as we examine Hildegard's way of healing), a self-ideal, and ethical convictions—all intertwined.[24]

The lifestyle of a person is focused on two central aspects: cognitive and motivational interaction. "Adlerian psychology is cognitive in that it clearly focuses upon the cognitive structures that underlie personality; it is psychodynamic in that it stresses not just

---

21. Jong, Mayke De. "INTRODUCTION." In *In Samuel's Image*, 1–15. Brill, 1996. https://doi.org/10.1163/9789004246614_002.
22. Kujawa-Holbrook, Sheryl A., trans. *Hildegard of Bingen: Essential Writings and Chants of a Christian Mystic—Annotated & Explained*. 1st edition. SkyLight Paths, 2016, xvi.
23. Esser, Annette. *The Hildegard of Bingen Pilgrimage Book*. Collegeville: Liturgical Press, 2022, 313.
24. Maniacci, Michael, and Harold Mosak. *Primer of Adlerian Psychology*. 1st edition. Hoboken: Routledge, 1999, 49.

cognitive bases of personality, but motivational issues…motivation is not caused by libido [as in Freud's theory], but rather the striving for significance."[25] However, a person is not completely stuck with their early observations and poor interpretations about the world from their childhood understanding in the family of origin.[26] Adler emphasized that "it is not what one has [psychologically] inherited that is important, but what one does with his inheritance."[27] Hildegard clearly does much with hers, as we can see in her life and healing approach.

Visions and Illnesses

Hildegard had visions from a very early age. The way that she was forced to cope with them influences her physical health and her sense of belonging. In her words:

> *In the third year of my life, I saw such a great light that my soul trembled, but, because of my youth, I could not speak about it. In the eighth year of my life, I was offered to God for my spiritual life. Up to my fifteenth year, I saw many things and told about them in such a simple way that those that heard them wondered where they came from and from whom they came. I myself also wondered why, while I was looking deeply into my soul, I retained the possibility of seeing other external things, and at the same time I wondered why I did not hear this from any other person. As a consequence, as much as possible, I kept secret the vision which I had seen in my soul.*[28]

---

25. Ibid., 50.
26. Ibid., 33.
27. Ibid., 24.
28. Fuhrkkotter, Adelgundis and Mary Palmquist, Mary. *The Life of the Holy Hildegard*. Edited by John Kulas. Complete Numbers Starting with 1, 1st edition. Liturgical Press, 1995, 50-51.

My Sap is Rising

At the age of seventy-nine, she described her experiences in a letter to Flemish monk Guibert of Gembloux:

From my early childhood, before my bones, nerves, and veins were fully strengthened, I have always seen this vision in my soul, even to the present time, when I am more than seventy years old. In this vision my soul, as God would have it, rises up high into the vault of heaven and into the changing sky and spreads itself out among different people, although they are far away from me in distant lands and places. And because I see them in this way in my soul, I observe them in accord with the shifting clouds and other created things. I do not hear them with my outward ears, nor do I perceive them by the thought of my heart or by any combination of my five senses, but in my soul alone, while my outward eyes are open. So I have never fallen prey to ecstasy in the visions, but I see them wide awake, day and night...

The light that I see thus is not spatial, but it is far, far brighter than a cloud that carries the sun. I can measure neither height, nor length, nor breadth in it; and I call it "the reflection of the living light." And as the sun, the moon, and the stars appear in water, so writings, sermons, virtues, and certain human actions take form for me and gleam within it.

Now whatever I have seen or learned in this vision remains in my memory for a long time, so that, when I have seen and heard it, I remember; and I see, hear, and know all at once, and as if in an instant I learn what I know...

Moreover, I can no more recognize the form of this light than I can gaze directly on the sphere of the sun. Sometimes—but not often—I see within this light another light, which I call "the Living Light." And I cannot describe when and how I see it, but while I see it, all sorrow and anguish leave me, so that then I feel like a simple girl instead of an old woman.[29]

---

29. Newman, Barbara. *Sister of Wisdom: St. Hildegard's Theology of the Feminine.* First

Danae Ashley, M.Div., M.A., LMFT

One story of Hildegard's childhood only found in the *Acta inquisitionis* (a canonization document) describes a conversation with her nurse about when Hildegard described an unborn calf which was to be "white and marked with different colored spots on its forehead, feet, and back." The nurse told Hildegard's mother, and Hildegard was rewarded with the calf when it was born exactly as she had envisioned it.[30]

Who were significant people in my life when I was growing up that influence the way I view the world today?

Hildegard seems to have had many people who cared for her as she grew up. Even with these relationships and her recurring illness from childhood, she could not entrust just anyone with what she saw. An example of how this influenced her lifestyle is through what Adler would call an Early Recollection—a memory that continues to influence our worldview. As she wrote in her *Vita*:

> *I did not come to know many other external things because of the frequent illnesses that I suffered from earliest days up to the present and which so weakened my body that my strength left me. When I became exhausted, I tried to find out from my nurse if she saw anything at all other than the usual external objects. And she answered: "Nothing," because she saw nothing like I did. Then I was seized with a great fear and did not dare to reveal this to anyone. While I spoke about all kinds of things, I took care to talk about future things.*[31]

Edition, With a New Preface, Bibliography, and Discography. Berkeley: University of California Press, 1998, 6-7.
30. Flanagan, Sabina. *Hildegard of Bingen: A Visionary Life*. 2nd edition. Hoboken: Routledge, 1998, 24.
31. Fuhrkkotter, Adelgundis and Mary Palmquist. *The Life of the Holy Hildegard*. Edited by John Kulas. Complete Numbers Starting with 1, 1st edition. Liturgical Press, 1995, 51.

Hildegard's illnesses were often tied to her visions. But which came first? Did she become ill because of being a conduit for God or did the visions come because she was ill? Various scholars and medical practitioners have attributed her visions to migraines or schizophrenia or an unknown neurological condition. From a spiritual perspective and from Hildegard's own embodied experience, she believed the visions were from God. Unlike other mystics such as St. Teresa of Avila or St. John of the Cross, Hildegard's goal was not union and ecstasy with God, but to share and teach God's messages that came through in what she often described as a waking state. Her openness of soul and self to being God's vessel through which these visions flowed clearly took great energy from her. While modern psychology wants to pathologize spiritual experience and encourage a mind/body/spirit split, that is not how Hildegard lived. In fact, it is not how I believe we should live.

In psychotherapy, we understand how much psychic and physical energy it takes to keep a secret from oneself or another, as well as to heal another, so it is not surprising that she would become ill after experiencing a vision and having to keep it to herself. How many of us have had this happen in our own lives? I have seen clients who are physically burdened with the secrets they have kept. Hildegard's fear of not fitting in the class- and role-structured world of her time kept her safe when she was a child but ultimately cost her as she grew into adulthood.

According to her *Vita*, Hildegard shared her visions with a small circle: Jutta and the monk, Volmar, in whom Jutta confided the secret. After Jutta's death, Hildegard continued to have visions into her forty-third year. At this point, she "was pressured by severe pains to reveal what I had seen and heard. Still, I was very fearful and ashamed to express what I had kept silent about for so long. My veins and my heart were at that point at full strength, something that had been lacking to me from childhood."[32] She was finally forced to personally share her visions with Volmar, and he

---

32. Fuhrkkotter, Adelgundis and Mary Palmquist. *The Life of the Holy Hildegard*.

encouraged her to write them down. After he studied them, Volmar confided in Abbot Kuno. With their support, she later sent letters to Bernard of Clairvaux and Pope Eugenius III requesting permission to continue to reveal what she saw from the 'Living Light'. With permission granted, she began to write her first work, *Scivias* ("Know the Ways" 1142-1151), a collection of 26 of her visions. As her visions continued, they were written down in what would become *Liber Vitae Meritorum* ("Book of Life's Merits" or "Book of the Rewards of Life" 1158-1163) and *Liber Divinorum Operum* ("Book of Divine Works" 1163/64-1172 or 1174) also known as *De operatione Dei* ("On God's Activity").

Adlerian Link

Here I would like to pause and consider Alfred Adler's lifestyle biological factors that are similar to Hildegard's. Adler was also from a large family. He was the second child of seven born on February 7, 1870, into a Jewish family in the outskirts of Vienna where they were a minority. Like Hildegard, Adler was frequently ill as a child, suffering from various illnesses including rickets, spasms of the glottis, pneumonia, and poor eyesight. At the tender age of three years old, one of Adler's siblings died next to him in bed.[33] While he did not see visions as Hildegard did, Adler's psychological theory is certainly influenced by these experiences, especially the ideas of belonging, inferiority, and weakness and how these influence a person's lifestyle. Adler wrote about what drew him to become a physician, which exemplifies these ideas:

When I was five, I became ill with pneumonia and was given up by the physician. A second physician advised a treatment just the same, and in a few days I became well again. In the joy over my

---

Edited by John Kulas. Complete Numbers Starting with 1, 1st edition. Liturgical Press, 1995, 51.
33. Maniacci, Michael, and Harold Mosak. *Primer of Adlerian Psychology*. 1st edition. Hoboken: Routledge, 1999, 1.

recovery, there was talk for a long time about the mortal danger in which I was supposed to have been. From that time on, I recall always thinking of myself in the future as a physician. This means that I had set a goal from which I could expect an end to my childlike distress, my fear of death. Clearly, I expected more from the occupation of my choice than it could accomplish: The overcoming of death and of the fear of death is something I should not have expected from human, but only from divine accomplishments. Reality, however, demands action, and so I was forced to modify my goal by changing the conscious form of the guiding fiction until it appeared to satisfy reality. So I came to choose the occupation of physician in order to overcome death and the fear of death.[34]

Like Adler, Hildegard was drawn to her various roles in life because of her striving to understand and overcome what was mysterious to her in childhood, while trying to maintain the safety, significance, and belonging that is vital to every being. Hildegard's organ inferiority—whatever system was weak in her body that created illness—forced her to compensate, just as Adler did, on a psychic level. Her lively mind and high energy drove her forward in her interests. Her private logic of not sharing her visions because of the responses she received from others meant that she could not always be her whole self in the world. The Adlerian concept of private logic is the way a person "behaves 'as if' their early learning were 'true' and set in stone ('concrete operations'). They set out to confirm their expectations and apply them in ever increasingly wider social fields."[35] These expectations can be modified as a person matures, but the core convictions remain unless they have a therapeutic experience through formal therapy or a life event.

---

34. Ansbacher, Heinz L., and Rowena R. Ansbacher, eds. *The Individual Psychology of Alfred Adler: A Systematic Presentation in Selections from His Writings.* Harper Perennial, 1964, 199.
35. Maniacci, Michael, and Harold Mosak. *Primer of Adlerian Psychology.* 1st edition. Hoboken: Routledge, 1999, 36.

Danae Ashley, M.Div., M.A., LMFT

Most people have heard of therapy, but a therapeutic life event may not be on one's radar. A good example of this is the Bible story of Saul of Tarsus in the ninth chapter of the Book of Acts verses 3-9. Saul was a persecutor of early Christians until he had a transformational experience on the road to Damascus through a vision of Jesus Christ.

Now as he was going along and approaching Damascus, suddenly a light from heaven flashed around him. He fell to the ground and heard a voice saying to him, 'Saul, Saul, why do you persecute me?' He asked, 'Who are you, Lord?' The reply came, 'I am Jesus, whom you are persecuting. But get up and enter the city, and you will be told what you are to do.' The men who were travelling with him stood speechless because they heard the voice but saw no one. Saul got up from the ground, and though his eyes were open, he could see nothing; so they led him by the hand and brought him into Damascus. For three days he was without sight, and neither ate nor drank.[36]

When his sight was restored by the power of God through the high priest Ananias, he was baptized, changed his name to Paul, and became an ardent apostle of Jesus.

Hildegard had her own transformational experience when she could no longer deny who she was, and the Living Light (God) compelled her to speak. Suddenly, her voice, and the Living Light through it, could not be stopped. She became her whole self when in alignment with the Living Light. This experience illustrates what happens physically and psychically when we heed that still, small, voice within. When we are congruent inside and out with the Living Light—or God, Higher Power, or whatever you wish to call it from your experience—our lives can be more than we could ask for or imagine. Hildegard truly believed, for herself and others, that

---

36. Attridge, Harold W., and Society of Biblical Literature. *HarperCollins Study Bible: Fully Revised & Updated.* HarperOne, 2006.

when one's spirit was in alignment with the Living Light, one had peace and purpose. It did not mean life was easier. We have only to look at Hildegard's many challenges to understand this truth. Think about it this way: Life is a river and occasionally there's a storm or minor tumult on the surface, but deep underneath the current flows with confidence to its destination. That is what Hildegard understood about the Living Light: there was deep peace even amidst the clamor. It could no longer be denied, and it was time for her to be whole.

Not heeding God's voice, as Hildegard discovered, meant that the body suffered. She would be unable to get out of bed for days and was sometimes paralyzed. Our bodies tell us when we are betraying ourselves and our values: "our bodies keep the score," as Dutch psychiatrist Bessel van der Kolk wrote in his book *The Body Keeps the Score*.[37] Hildegard herself is a case study for this, but we can also look at real life examples in ourselves and in the people around us. This is not only about how trauma is stored in our bodies, but even more deeply how we listen to the Living Light, who created us to be whole.

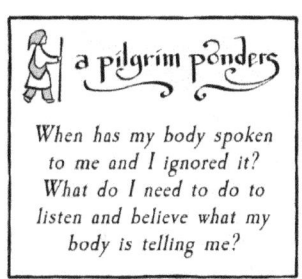

a pilgrim ponders

When has my body spoken to me and I ignored it? What do I need to do to listen and believe what my body is telling me?

Before I left on my pilgrimage to Hildegard's land, I felt heavy, both in spirit and in body. As the initial shock wore off, my grief over leaving my congregation so suddenly settled onto me like a weighted blanket, and not a cozy one. I also had to have foot surgery to remove three screws from a previous bunion surgery six weeks before I embarked on my journey. My body and my spirit were exhausted. I could not identify what I needed or when I needed it. Like a good product of Western culture's Protestant work ethic, I pushed through, letting my anxiety about money and my

---

37. van der Kolk, Bessel. *The Body Keeps the Score: Brain, Mind, and Body in the Healing of Trauma*. Reprint edition. New York, NY: Penguin Books, 2015.

future fuel me even as I was on the verge of collapse. If I had not scheduled the pilgrimage at the time I arranged it, I know I would have completely broken down.

Instead, the liminal time on pilgrimage, learning about Hildegard and her land, aided in anchoring my spirit and body within myself again. I was able to create a pace that worked for me so that I was not intellectually overwhelmed with foreign language, culture, and rules, as well as resting as much as I needed to each night. I also listened to my body's wisdom and rented a car for the second part of my time so that my foot would not be overstrained and would heal properly. If I had kept going the way I had been going before, I am certain I would have become ill. That is usually my body's way of saying *You've ignored all my signs to slow down and now I'm not going to let you ignore me any longer.* When this happens, I pay attention really quick.

An Adlerian viewpoint asserts that physical symptoms can be one (but not the only) response to a psychological event and these symptoms serve a purpose. Adler believed that organ inferiority predisposes a person to break down when undergoing stress and it affects the physiological point of the most vulnerability.[38] This is clear in Hildegard's story. As she stated that she had been ill since infancy, this was her organ inferiority weakness. Anytime her visions came, the stress of the visions and of keeping them to herself invited illness. It could be argued that in some cases, her symptoms of illness also served her to get her way, such as when she took ill until Abbot Kuno relented when she wanted to leave Disibodenberg and found her own monastery at Rupertsberg.

Many of us have our own experiences of the body expressing our stress. I know people who have herpes outbreaks or autoimmune flares when they have been under too much stress and not nurturing their bodies with healthy food, movement, and sleep. The outbreak or flare up is a physical sign from their body that they

---

38. Maniacci, Michael, and Harold Mosak. *Primer of Adlerian Psychology*. 1st edition. Hoboken: Routledge, 1999, 119.

need to slow down and reconnect to themselves, others, and the Living Light. I have also witnessed people making themselves physically ill because they wanted to avoid something. Instead of slowing down and making those connections within so they could ask for what they really wanted from a secure place, the illness allowed them to get what they wanted, but at the cost of congruence. Lifestyle is adaptable until it encounters an event in which it is ill-prepared and then we must make a choice on how we respond —consciously or unconsciously.[39]

The Importance of Place

Think about where you lived as a child and adolescent. How do those places influence the way you see the world? We cannot overlook the importance of the external environment in which Hildegard grew up and how it influenced her future work and visions. This is the *Weltbild* I mentioned earlier in this chapter. In her formative years with her family of origin, as well as her time with Jutta in Sponheim before they entered life in the anchorite cell at Disibodenberg, Hildegard was able to enjoy the lush farmland, vineyards, wooded hills, and rivers of the Rhine Valley. Even the walk with Jutta and the other young woman to the great Benedictine monastery of Disibodenberg to be sealed in their anchorage would have been full of natural beauty.

In Hildegard's time, Disibodenberg was always under construction, and it commanded the hilltop at the crux of the River Nahe and the River Glan. The view encompasses miles of farmland and vineyards, as well as villages that the monastery owned or worked closely with. The three young women formed a female community amidst the male monks, and their environment was limited to the stone walls, dirt floor, and a small window to pass things through and let a glimpse of sky and light in, until they moved quarters many years later.

---

39. Ibid., 122.

Danae Ashley, M.Div., M.A., LMFT

Hildegard, with her quick and vigorous mind and her experience of visions, went from being free to connect with creation around her to keeping the memory of those sights alive within her as she sought the spiritual, internal realm of prayer, psalm singing, and quiet within the anchorage. It is no surprise then that when she finally wrote down her visions in *Scivias* they were ripe with images of lush creation and the interconnectedness of it all.

In the Christian tradition, God uses the incarnation of a person to do God's work, primarily their personality and experiences of the world around them. As the 19th century Episcopal preacher Phillips Brooks once said, "Preaching is truth mediated through personality." Hildegard was preaching with the Voice of the Living Light through her visions, and the Living Light used her personality and experiences to communicate the message. The images she used in her visions were certainly unique in many ways, but when she speaks about creation and she talks about *viriditas*—the greening spirit—for healing, she is writing a love letter to the Rhine Valley. Her images would be very different if she was a desert mother or had a hermitage of ice and snow.

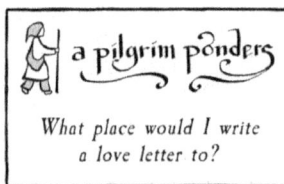

a pilgrim ponders

What place would I write a love letter to?

Place matters in the human psyche and the way we view and engage with the world. Adler applied the psychology of use to environmental influences and heredity with the question of *Who uses it?* As he wrote:

> *The raw material with which the Individual Psychologist works is: The relationship of the individual to the problems of the outside world. The Individual Psychologist has to observe how a particular individual relates himself to the outside world. This outside world includes the individual's own body, his bodily functions, and the functions of his mind. He does not relate himself to the outside world in a predetermined manner as is often assumed. He relates*

himself always according to his own interpretation of himself and of his present problem. His limits are not only the common human limits, but also the limits he has set himself. It is neither heredity nor environment that determines his relationship to the outside world. Heredity only endows him with certain abilities. Environment only gives him certain impressions. These abilities and impressions, and the manner in which he "experiences" them — that is to say, the interpretation he makes of these experiences — are the bricks that he uses in his own "Creative" way to build up his attitude toward life. It is his individual way of using these bricks — or in other words, it is his attitude toward life — that determines his relationship to the outside world (Adler, 1935, p. 5).[40]

Hildegard seemingly set limits on herself around her visions, showing deference to Jutta until after Jutta died. Finally, in her early 40s, Hildegard began to step out into the sunlight once again.

Light as a Feather

After spending a couple of hours wandering through the Disibodenberg, I found myself on the *Meditationsweg* (Meditation Path) on the right side of the hill. Accepting the invitation to walk prayerfully, I encountered signs with Scripture and sayings from Hildegard on them. I imagined what this path might have led to during Hildegard's time. It was probably not meditative because of all the construction work being done when she lived there. Now, though, it was quiet, with the only work being done in my heart and soul.

The path spilled out into a clearing with an ancient oak commanding the view in the midst of vineyards leading down to the valley. I placed my hand on its sun-warmed trunk and thought

---

40. "Heredity (Genetic Possibility)/Environment (Environmental Opportunity) | AdlerPedia." Accessed November 7, 2024. https://www.adlerpedia.org/concepts/112.

Danae Ashley, M.Div., M.A., LMFT

about all the seasons and people it had seen come and go. Looking out across the varied hues of green and through the oak's branches spread through the blue of the sky, I realized there were no limitations for me any longer. I was free to answer God's call wholly—no longer tied to an institutional system's needs. I joined Hildegard as I stepped into the sunlight, light as a feather on the breath of God.

Pilgrim's Reflection

All exercises under the Pilgrim's Reflection section are for personal and group reflection. Every group has a different dynamic, and the leader can decide which of the exercises they wish to use based on the needs of their group.

1. A genogram is a basic family tree tool in family systems therapy used to understand the family constellation and family atmosphere. I invite you to create your own genogram. There are a variety of ways to create this that you can find online, or follow the simple instructions below:

- Start with your grandparents on each side, then your parents and their siblings (and their spouses) on the next level, and finally you and your siblings (and spouses). Note any divorce, separation, or death.
- Write down health issues, education levels, sexuality, economics, spirituality, abuse of any kind, and any other questions you may have for each person.
- Draw straight lines connecting you to who you feel closest to and jagged lines for who you feel in conflict with.
- Take a look and see if there are any patterns. What do you want to take with you from your family of origin? What do you want to leave behind? How have these patterns influenced you?
- What will it take to intentionally make a change? Write down one or two baby steps. You may wish to share these with others for accountability.

Danae Ashley, M.Div., M.A., LMFT

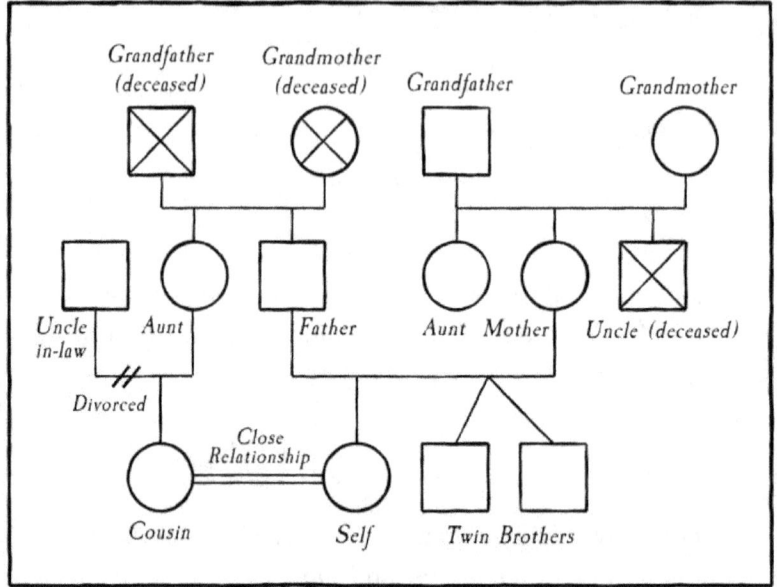

Sample Genogram

2. Every person has their own worldview based on their experience of life. Many times, hidden expectations based on your worldview show up in friendships and romantic relationships, creating conflict. What is your *Weltbild*—your worldview? What are your ideas about life and the world?

Here are some Adlerian writing prompts to help you explore this concept and bring what may be hidden into consciousness:

- I am…
- I ought to…
- Women/Men/Nonbinary people should…
- People are…
- Good people should…
- The world is…(including ideas of nature and the external world)
- School/Work/Government is…(you can explore each separately)

3. How has living in a particular place influenced your outlook on life?

4. Hildegard came from a large family, with a number who entered the Church in some way, including nieces and nephews. We have a letter to her brother, Hugo, that admonishes him for being in conflict with their brother, Roricus. Hildegard is always direct (and bossy), which may seem shocking to the modern reader. However, she was committed to transforming the world through the Living Light and called out for reform whether it was with a Pope, a Bishop, or her brothers.

> *The Church frequently recounts miracles, but sometimes they move beyond truth into derision. Therefore, I admonish you not to accuse your brother Roricus unjustly in your heart and not to move beyond the bounds in speaking evil words about him. God knows that you are not acting correctly in this matter.*
>
> *Therefore, beware lest the Lord find you guilty in this wrath of yours and other similar matters. May God have mercy on you in all your sins.*[41]

Imagine that Hildegard wrote this letter to you about a sibling or chosen family member. How would you reply? Is there someone with whom you need to make amends?

---

41. Baird, Joseph L., ed. *The Personal Correspondence of Hildegard of Bingen*. 1st edition. New York: Oxford University Press, 2006, 96.

Danae Ashley, M.Div., M.A., LMFT

Benediction

The following is a hymn Hildegard wrote about St. Disibod and the way God worked through him to attract many followers of Christ. Considering this and the land where he lived, she gives him the name "Greenness of God's Finger." [42]

Group option: One person leads while the group says the response.

Leader
Greenness of God's finger,
through you God has planted a vineyard
that gleams on high
like a carved pillar.

Response
You are glorious in God's preparation.

Leader
O height of the mountain
You shall never be brought low
In God's judgment.
Yet you stand in the distance
Like an exile.
But there is no armed power
To seize you.

Response
You are glorious [in] God's preparation.

Symphonia (Songs) 42

---

42. Kujawa-Holbrook, Sheryl A., translator. *Hildegard of Bingen: Essential Writings and Chants of a Christian Mystic—Annotated & Explained.* 1st edition, SkyLight Paths, 2016, 81.

Chapter 2
Holism
A Gardener's Approach

The sun broke through the clouds as I wound my way through the country roads of the verdant Rhine River valley seeking what I had started to call my next "spiritual geocaching location." With *The Hildegard of Bingen Pilgrimage Book* as my guide, I tried, mostly successfully, to find the next tableau on the trail. My gray Hyundai Kona rental car drove like a dream as I meandered through the fields of wheat, vineyards, and forest. There was so much vegetation to drink in, I thought I might turn the color of a new blade of grass just by breathing the air.

Having established how vital place was to Hildegard and her worldview, especially her healing, it will not surprise you to know one of the things that struck me the most on Pilgrimage Way was how lush and alive the places where Hildegard grew up and ministered were. Some of the farms and vineyards date back to Roman times. Everywhere I turned, things were green and growing, the fecundity of the earth celebrated in every direction.

As I drove, I listened with keen interest to the audiobook version of Dr. Victoria Sweet's *God's Hotel*, read by the author. I became an immediate fan and later reached out to Dr. Sweet to talk about my research for this book. I think Hildegard would have enjoyed her sharp mind and generous spirit immensely.

Dr. Sweet shares her story of being a physician at Laguna Honda Hospital in San Francisco and her discovery of Hildegard when she began to study premodern medicine. I resonated with the holistic care she tried to give patients in a healthcare system that was moving further and further from this approach. As an Adlerian psychotherapist, I have faced the challenges of a healthcare system directed by insurance companies, focused on diagnoses and a 50-minute hour and not what the patient needs for healing and wholeness. You will not be surprised to know that I do not accept insurance at my practice. I want to spend my time, like Hildegard, focusing on my patient and what is happening in their whole life, not doing paperwork and battling multimillion dollar corporations to get paid less than valued, while billing insurance to scratch out a living wage.[1]

Following in Hildegard's footsteps doing holistic medicine when it comes to mental health means the shape of my practice and approach looks different than other colleagues. I contemplated this while looking at the flashes of green out my window and wondered how this pilgrimage would bring even more clarity to how I viewed myself as a psychotherapist and deepen my work with clients.

Slow Medicine

What Dr. Sweet calls Hildegard's 'Way of Medicine'[2] begins with the assumption that a person is first and foremost striving for alignment with God, the Living Light. This is the foundation of what I am calling Hildegard's psychotherapeutic approach: When one's

---

1. I have many excellent colleagues who are paneled (have contracts) with insurance companies. This works for them and I am glad. We need everyone and there is room for all approaches. Accessibility to good mental health care is hard enough to find and being able to use insurance is a Godsend for many. However, there are other methods of accessibility when not paneled with insurance, such as superbills and sliding scale fees, that I find successful.

2. Sweet, Victoria. *God's Hotel: A Doctor, a Hospital, and a Pilgrimage to the Heart of Medicine.* Reprint edition. Riverhead Books, 2013.

soul is in alignment with the Living Light, one has peace and purpose, resulting in the health of body, mind, and soul. Consider, as you read this chapter, what spiritual alignment feels like to you.

In *God's Hotel*, Dr. Sweet describes how she decided to study *Causae et Curae* as if she were one of Hildegard's 12th century students. She slowly began to understand Hildegard's "Way of Medicine" that was amid Hildegard's descriptions of diseases, diagnoses, and treatments.

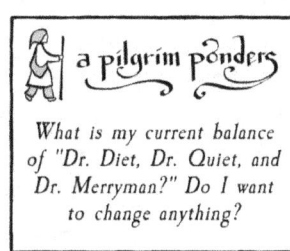

a pilgrim ponders

What is my current balance of "Dr. Diet, Dr. Quiet, and Dr. Merryman?" Do I want to change anything?

Dr. Sweet concluded that after careful observation of the patient—vital signs, general well-being, social connections, environment, and story—Hildegard would come up with an individualized prescription for treatment. This was a rule for living summarized by the adage: "Even without a doctor/You have three doctors at hand/Dr. Diet, Dr. Quiet, and Dr. Merryman."[3]

In modern terms, Dr. Diet represents what one should eat and drink; Dr. Quiet represents how much physical movement, sleep, and rest one should partake; and Dr. Merryman represents low stress levels, what kind and how much pleasure should be had (sex, for instance), and regulation of emotions. After this regime was prescribed, an herbal mixture or other medicine would be given, often in conjunction with prayer and/or ritual. Then came the waiting and perhaps adjustments until the person was cured or, as Hildegard puts it, "It is God's will for him to die." Yes, you read that right. Die. Remember, in Hildegard's worldview it was at God's pleasure that people lived or died. This understanding also protected the practitioner from trying a cure and having it fail.

Hildegard was placed well to learn and understand healing. At the large, bustling monastery of Disibodenberg where she likely

---

3. Inquirer. "Doctor Diet, Doctor Quiet and Doctor Merryman." *Journal of the American Medical Association* XXIII, no. 19 (November 10, 1894): 732–732. https://doi.org/10.1001/jama.1894.02421240030012.

served in the infirmary, people from all over the area, not just the nuns and monks, would come for healing. The patients were surrounded by people singing their prayers throughout the day, knowing they were held by community even if they were on their sickbed. Plants were grown for food and for tinctures, salves, and remedies, some of them distinctly medieval—boil a wolf anyone? Hildegard applied the best of medieval holism: watching, observing, and listening for what works for someone's body and adjusting for what doesn't—looking at the whole person.

Dr. Sweet talks about Hildegard's holistic approach to medicine as akin to being a gardener. As I listened while I drove through the countryside, I thought about the various Hildegard gardens along the Pilgrimage Way that included plants from her time which we use for healing and health in contemporary alternative and complementary medicine today such as lavender, chamomile, peppermint, sage, marjoram, costmary, juniper, and many others. Hildegard studied not only how plants could heal, but also the aspects of plants that made them alive. This reminded me of the Master Gardener classes that I took through the partnership of Washington State University and our county.[4] Learning to troubleshoot plant problems, we would first observe what was physically wrong with the leaves, stem, and flowers (if they had any). If it wasn't an obvious bug or other predator, we would look at the soil, how much light it was getting, and how much water. Then we would try something to improve the conditions. Dr. Sweet likened Hildegard's approach to healing to a gardener treating a plant. Adjust this and that, then watch and wait. Give the plant time and space to heal. Adjust as needed. The same goes for people. When applied now, this type of approach is considered slow medicine.

---

4. This program is in every U.S. state through a partnership with their state university and the local counties. I highly recommend it for anyone who wants to learn about their local environment and gardening responsibly. It also brings you into community (good for mental health!) with others who are interested in gardening and requires volunteering in the wider community (plant clinics, demonstration gardens, etc.).

Adlerian Link

The basis of Adler's Individual Psychology is just that: individual. Like Hildegard, his focus on holism is primary. He believed that each person is indivisible—our body, mind, and emotions work together to strive for our final, fictional goal. Why fictional? Adler puts it this way:

Very early in my work, I found man to be a [self-consistent] unity. The foremost task of Individual Psychology is to prove this unity in each individual—in his thinking, feeling, acting, in his so-called conscious and unconscious, in every expression of his personality.[5] *The [fictional] goal can well be understood as a teleological device of the soul which seeks orientation.*[6]

The fictional final goal was, for Adler, "the principle of internal, subjective *causation* of psychological events."[7] For many people, it is often (not always) about belonging. Adler adapted this from the "As If" philosophy of Hans Vaihinger. Jane Griffith and Robert L. Powers define this concept clearly:

Fictional goal, guiding fiction, and fictional finalism are related terms referring to the same feature of psychological compensation, namely, the individual's unconscious, subjectively conceived, ever-present goal of success, the self-ideal. In the first few years of life, the child creates a fictional goal of success that contrasts to and assuages the child's intolerable feelings of inferiority, evident in the phrase, "Some day when I grow up…" As the person develops, the goal

---

5. Ansbacher, Heinz L., and Rowena R. Ansbacher, eds. *The Individual Psychology of Alfred Adler: A Systematic Presentation in Selections from His Writings.* Harper Perennial, 1964, 175.
6. Ibid., 93.
7. "Fictional Goal/Guiding Fiction/Fictional Finalism | AdlerPedia." Accessed November 8, 2024. https://www.adlerpedia.org/concepts/45.

continues to operate as a guiding fiction in any present situation. It gives direction to the person's movement, while shifting to new forms of concretization in the ambitions of adult life; "Only when I am _____ (good, rich, smart, important, in control, etc.), will I be _____ (admired, accepted, secure, significant, etc.)."[8]

For psychotherapists, awareness of the final, fictional goal "enables us to understand the hidden meaning behind the various separate acts and to see them as parts of a whole."[9] In Adler's view, every behavior serves a purpose, and the purpose is one or more fictional goals. One way we can examine how our behaviors are serving our final, fictional goal is through examining what Adler called 'Life Tasks.' The Life Tasks were Work, Love, and Social Tasks. For example, if we rate each Task on a scale of 1-10 with 1 being the worst and 10 being the best, we can see which Task needs encouragement and can take small steps to improve it. If we do not understand each part of the whole, we cannot assist in healing.

What would Adler make of the Living Light when it comes to healing? Although Adler does not include spirituality in his initial Life Tasks, he writes and speaks about it throughout his work. Followers of Adler have added several other Life Tasks, including the Spiritual Task, to Adler's initial Work, Love, and Social Tasks. Holism, in Adler's view, is not just the indivisibility of self, but also the connection one has to others and creation through social embeddedness that he called *Gemeinschaftsgefühl* or community spirit. Hildegard shares this same idea, which is expressed through her visions.

Adler was born Jewish and converted to Christianity when he was 34 years old. This was not a passionate conversion, but most likely in response to feeling that the exclusiveness of Judaism went against his ideal of social interest, as well as a desire for profes-

---

8. Ibid., Accessed November 8, 2024.
9. Ansbacher & Ansbacher, op. cit., 92-93.

sional assimilation in Viennese society. Psychologically, Adler found a belief in God—no matter from which religious tradition—to be helpful, as he wrote:

> *The idea of God and its immense significance for mankind can be understood and appreciated from the viewpoint of Individual Psychology as concretization and interpretation of the human recognition of greatness and perfection, and as commitment of the individual as well as society to a goal which rests in man's future and which in the present heightens the driving force by enhancing the feelings and emotions.*[10]

I wonder, based on what we know of Hildegard's origins and early life in the anchorage, if her fictional, final goal was about belonging? As a cloistered nun with a powerful mind and high energy, we see multiple instances of the way she ensured her own belonging even when stepping out. Hildegard's ideal goal (as opposed to fictional) was focused on being in alignment with the Living Light and having inner and outer congruence. Her belonging and significance were not dependent on imperfect humanity but on God, and she discovered many concrete ways to serve this purpose. The conflict of not being her true self came to fruition when God demanded that she write down her visions—that she fully embraced who she was created to be. At the same time, she followed her fictional, final goal for belonging in her various communities by using her intellect and her nobility to be politically savvy, care for her fellow nuns, and stay alive in a tumultuous time in German history.

---

10. Ansbacher, Heinz L., and Rowena R. Ansbacher, eds. *The Individual Psychology of Alfred Adler: A Systematic Presentation in Selections from His Writings.* Harper Perennial, 1964, 276.

Danae Ashley, M.Div., M.A., LMFT

Viriditas

The Wallfahrtskirche, or pilgrim church, of St. Hildegard und St. Johannes der Täufer in Rüdesheim am Rhein, halfway between the town of Rüdesheim and Eibingen Abbey, was the site of the second monastery that Hildegard founded across the Rhine from her first monastery at Rupertsberg. While the monastery no longer exists, the walls around the grounds, as well as monuments in the church's floor, date back to Hildegard's time.

When I first stepped into the sanctuary, I did not know what to expect. My eye was first drawn to the large image of Hildegard's 'Blue Man'[11] above the altar. Hildegard had a vision of a "man in sapphire blue" whom she called Christ who is present in everything. Part of her vision of the Trinity, he stands in the center of a circle of dark gold with lines that look like the rings in a cross-section of a tree. This circle is inside a larger, pale-yellow circle with the same rings, all placed on a dark blue background with yellow, light blue, and red designs in between a green border.

It is a strange, almost primitive image when you see it for the first time in her work of visions, *Scivias*, or online, but I was a wee bit awestruck to see it above the altar. It was not the image of Christ I was expecting. Then again, nothing about this pilgrimage or my life at that time was what I had been expecting. I often remind my clients that God is doing a new thing and that if we are open to the

---

11. 'Blue Man' Image on this page: Fol. 047 of the Rupertsberg Scivias Codex of Saint Hildegard of Bingen, around 1175, original lost since 1945, hand copy on parchment 1930, Abbey of St. Hildegard, Rüdesheim-Eibingen.

My Sap is Rising

Holy Spirit, God opens our lives more than we could ask for or imagine, and once again I had to practice what I preached.

After pausing for a moment to take in the Christ image, my eyes caught the twinkle of light bouncing off gold—real gold. I gasped. On the altar was a large intricately decorated reliquary box containing Hildegard's relics. I felt the sensation of champagne bubbles rising up —a sparkling aliveness—through my torso and tears immediately sprang to my eyes. I walked toward the altar with prayers of thanksgiving on my lips, asking God what was needed of me. It was clear to me that Hildegard was present in a spiritual way and that I needed to follow her.

Like other mystical experiences I have had, this all happened simultaneously and quickly. I call this combination of sensations the "my sap is rising" experience. It is a sure sign that I am aligned with the Divine and that there is some new dance I am being invited into. I felt this when I accepted my call to ordination (after I ran from it for a while), when I decided not to pursue having children after a painful almost six-year fertility struggle with recurrent loss, when I learned about the Master Gardener program, and at other times—great and small.

I lit a candle at one of the side chapels, went up the steps to the reliquary, and prayed. It was enclosed in a clear glass box and the altar itself was surrounded by a simple length of chain so you could not touch it, but you could observe it. Below it, under the altar in mosaic was the phrase 'Heilige Hildegard bitte für uns 1098-1179'. *Holy Hildegard pray for us.* My sensations continued as I read this and I felt her presence. I particularly needed prayer for healing and courage—both of which Hildegard inspired.

As I left the church to continue my path up to Eibingen Abbey, my thoughts were drawn to how my mystical experience was akin to what I thought Hildegard meant by *viriditas*. To literally feel the sap rising in body and spirit was *viriditas* helping me heal.

What is Viriditas?

Viriditas is an important concept in Hildegard's psychotherapy and is related to how carefully she observed creation. She was not the first person to use this term. Before and during her lifetime, it could signify:

1. <u>Greenness</u>: The color itself.
2. <u>Green Sap</u>: The name for the humor of plants. In Hildegard's time, colors represented the elements: Black is the earth; Yellow is water; Yellow + Black = Green. When observing a plant, as the stem grew, it brought forth life force depicted in corresponding colors: Black (seed in Earth) to Yellow (sprouting stem) to Green (full growth) to Red (beginning to disintegrate) to Black (end of life cycle and return to Earth). See illustration below.
3. <u>Spiritual Way</u>: God/Divine spirit. Hildegard took the concept of *viriditas* as greenness and virility in nature and wedded it to the Divine presence in life, especially in later years.[12]

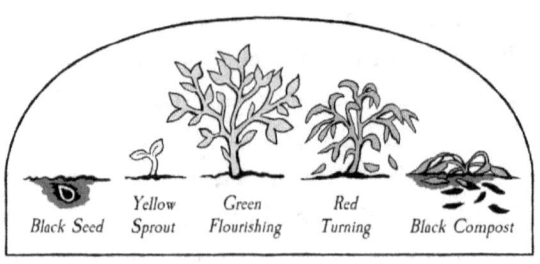

---

12. Sweet, Victoria. *Rooted in the Earth, Rooted in the Sky*. 1st edition. New York, NY: Routledge, 2006.

My Sap is Rising

To Hildegard, alignment with God flowed naturally into her understanding of *viriditas* and how it applies to healing. This is about a person's 'sap' and whether it is strong, weak, flowing, or blocked. Again, this reiterates the basis of Hildegard's psychotherapy: When one's soul is in alignment with the Living Light, one has peace and purpose, resulting in the health of body, mind, and soul. This 'Greening Spirit' comes first from God and when we can tap into it, it aids our healing.

Returning to our gardening metaphor, Hildegard would have been attentive to what was blocking the *viriditas* in a plant and her human patients. Would a plant need a different location? More water? Less sun? Would a person need rest for a bone to heal? Nourishing foods? More connection to God? In healing, Hildegard's ultimate question was to examine, "What is blocking your *viriditas* from healing your body, mind, and soul?" "What is in the way of *viriditas?*" or to put it yet another way, "What can you do to support your *viriditas* to aid you in healing?" She did not explicitly say or write this, but her actions embody it. This question is helpful both in body and mental health.

Adler also had a way at getting to this information so that he could understand the psychological purpose of the symptoms. He called it 'The Question': What would you be doing if these symptoms or problems were removed? From Hildegard's perspective, what would your *viriditas* look like if it were free to flow? And Adler's follow-up questions: If you weren't hiding behind this symptom, how would you be exposed? What scares you about that?

I think Hildegard would approve of Adler's questions. The ministry of presence shines through each of their approaches. Being fully attentive to another's story—to their distress and to their joy—brings both people closer to wholeness. There has never been a time when bearing witness to a parishioner or client's story has not moved me to be in touch with those parts of myself. My own *viriditas* responds with my greening spirit rising toward the other. It is good for each of us to have a few close people in our lives with

Danae Ashley, M.Div., M.A., LMFT

whom we can explore these deep and vulnerable places, whether it is a priest/pastor, therapist, friend, and/or family. Hildegard had Jutta, Volmar, the nun Richardis, and, of course, the Living Light.

Pilgrim's Reflection

1. What is your experience with gardening? How could you apply this 'slow medicine' metaphor to your own mental health? Do you need to make some adjustments?

2. How has nature been a healing place for you?

3. What is your final, fictional goal? As Harold Mosak and Michael Maniacci summarize:

> A final, fictional goal that organizes behavior is selected *unconsciously*, and skills that reinforce movement toward that goal are emphasized, and those that subjectively appear to be irrelevant are discarded.[13]

> I invite you to discover your final, fictional goal by filling in the blanks of this sentence:

> Only when I am_____(perfect, smart enough, rich, thin, in control, important, etc.), will I be_____(loved, accepted, secure, significant, cared for, etc.).

> Consider how this behavior has helped you and how it has hindered you in getting what you need. What are some of the skills that you have developed to reinforce movement toward your final, fictional goal? When you were a child, what do you wish would have been different? How would your feelings and behavior change if you felt safety, significance, and belonging just by being you?

---

13. Maniacci, Michael, and Harold Mosak. *Primer of Adlerian Psychology*. 1st edition. Hoboken: Routledge, 1999, 42.

4. Hildegard's question for healing was to examine: *"What is blocking your viriditas from healing your body, mind, and soul?"*

> To get to this answer, I invite you to consider what Alfred Adler called the 'Life Tasks'. On a scale of 1 to 10, you will rate how you feel you are doing in each Life Task, with 1 being the worst and 10 being the best.
>
> Work_____
> Social (Friendship/Community)_____
> Love_____
> Self_____
> Spirit_____
>
> After you finish rating each Life Task, choose one and reflect on how you could take a small step and improve it just one half or a full number higher. Make a goal date to check in with yourself about this step.

5. Witnessing the Dryness and Stagnation

> In order to allow the sap to rise and support our *viriditas* in healing, it is helpful to reflect on what our barriers are. Where do we need to prune—to let go—so that our *viriditas* can use that energy for healing and growth? Here are some writing prompts that are adapted from my former Adlerian professor, Sue Pye Brokaw, that are useful for reflection:
>
> - I felt *emotion* about/around/when *behavior*.
>   - The person(s) involved should not be named. The focus is on your emotion around a particular behavior. For example, "I felt *hurt and frustrated* when *I received complaints about the event after I asked others to help and they did not.*"

- When I *do this behavior*, I am avoiding *emotion or activity*.
    - For example, When I *binge watch Netflix for 8 hours*, I am avoiding *having a difficult conversation with my friend*.
- When I think about *a particular relationship*, it feels dry and or/stagnant. I believe this is because *the reason your intuition gives you*.
    - For example, When I think about *my sister*, it feels dry and stagnant. I believe this is because *we have both become busy in our lives and are not being intentional about staying close*.
- When this is completed, take a few moments of quiet time to acknowledge the emotions you've experienced and reflect on why the behaviors affected you in those particular ways. Did it remind you of something that happened when growing up? Does it remind you of something that happens at work? How can you invite your *viriditas*—the greening and growing of body, mind, and spirit—into your healing?
- Be gentle with yourself as you name these emotions and behaviors. Naming these things will be helpful in releasing them so they no longer control you or cast a shadow on your experience of life any longer.

Danae Ashley, M.Div., M.A., LMFT

Benediction

I invite you to embody your own *viriditas* in this portion of Hildegard's hymn, *O nobilissima viriditas*:[14]

> O most noble greenness,
> you are rooted in the sun,
> and in bright serenity you shine in a wheel
> that no earthly excellence comprehends,
> you are surrounded by embraces of divine mysteries.
> You redden like the dawn
> and you burn like the flame of the sun...
> [Viriditas! Viriditas!] (my addition)

---

14. Esser, Annette. *The Hildegard of Bingen Pilgrimage Book*. Liturgical Press, 2022.

Group/embodied option: Take turns saying a line, with all saying the final line together. You can follow the illustration on the next page or the instructions below.

> O most noble greenness (*Bow head, hands in prayer position.*)
> you are rooted in the sun, (*Bend to touch the earth, looking down until 'sun' then look up.*)
> and in bright serenity you shine in a wheel (*Rise up and slowly spin in a circle, raising your arms and hands up toward the sky.*)
> that no earthly excellence comprehends, (*Put fingers on the side of the head at each temple and turn head left and right.*)
> you are surrounded by embraces of divine (*Arms out wide, then embrace left,*)
> mysteries. (*Embrace middle and right.*)
> You redden like the dawn (*Lunge with left leg and left arm extended toward the center. Return.*)
> and you burn like the flame of the sun. (*Lunge with right leg and right arm extended toward the center. Return.*)
>
> Viriditas! Viriditas! (*Extend arms into a 'V' toward the sky at the first "Viriditas" and return to the beginning prayer position at the second.*

Danae Ashley, M.Div., M.A., LMFT

O, most noble greenness,   you are rooted in the   sun.

And in bright serenity you shine in a wheel   that no earthly excellence   comprehends.

You are surrounded   by embraces   of divine   mysteries.

You redden like the dawn   and you burn like the flame of the sun

 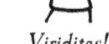

Viriditas!   Viriditas!

Chapter 3
Vices and Virtues
A Recipe for Healing

When I arrived at the Frankfurt airport, I had been traveling for hours on two different flights, and I was ready to go to the hotel to rest and get my bearings. It was a Holiday Inn, and I booked it because it was an airport hotel that had a shuttle. So, there I was, waiting in the shuttle line as bus after bus passed me. Finally, I saw the words 'Holiday Inn' on a shuttle. I waved them down like a drowning person desperate for help and I hopped on, relieved that I was finally going to get settled.

As I looked out the window at this new German landscape, I mused about what this adventure was going to be like and wondered who I would meet and what I would learn. I looked at my cell phone and saw that we had been driving for about 20 minutes—longer than I thought it would take. When we arrived shortly thereafter, I was reassured. It looked normal, if a little far from the airport. I grabbed my purple backpack and went to check-in.

There were several young German men working at the check-in counter and when I asked if any spoke English, one of them came forward to handle my reservation. I told him I had been traveling for almost 24 hours and was looking forward to resting. He made a

Danae Ashley, M.Div., M.A., LMFT

sympathetic sound and asked for my name and confirmation information. I gave it to him and as he typed into the computer, I looked around at the comfortable, quiet lounge nearby with a fireplace and a small restaurant. His voice brought back my attention, "I am sorry. We do not have your reservation," he told me apologetically. My heart dropped into my stomach. This was the type of thing I was afraid would happen. I was alone in a foreign country where I did not speak the language (aside from the translation app on my phone) and I was so tired I wanted to cry.

I had printed everything out in case my phone died or was stolen, so I showed him the front page of the printout to see if that offered any clues. He took one look at it and broke into a compassionate smile. "Ohhhhhhh," he said. "This is for the Holiday *Inn* and we are the Holiday Inn *Express*. You will need to get back on the shuttle when it returns and catch their shuttle at the airport. It won't have 'Express' on the side." I was so exhausted that I never even noticed that the first shuttle *had* 'Express' on the side.

The next shuttle would not be there for another 20 minutes, so they kindly made me some tea while I waited. I sat by the fire and messaged my husband to let him know that I had taken a wrong turn, but these gentle angels disguised as young men had gotten me back on the right path. They even gave me a couple of cookies with my tea, which soothed my weary body and soul, both being even happier an hour later when I checked into the correct hotel and they pulled up my reservation without a hitch. I went straight to my room, took a shower to get the travel grime off me, and promptly went to sleep with gratitude.

Life can be like that. We are distracted by the wrong things—like anxiety from being out of control—and don't notice when we stray from the track. It takes refocusing our attention to what is important, and sometimes the kindness of strangers, to find our way again.

The Soul's Journey

Imagine that you are in the visiting room at Rupertsberg with Hildegard. She has learned about your family constellation, environment, and what is blocking your *viriditas*.

Now she begins to formulate a prescription for you. How have you strayed from your path? This must begin with your connection with the Living Light. Some of the things blocking your *viriditas* have to do with Vices that are blocking your soul's pilgrimage to God as illustrated in the illumination on this page.[1] Hildegard knows just what to prescribe: she wants you to attend her morality play called *Ordo Virtutum (Order of the Virtues)*,[2] which tells the story of the soul's journey to God, following the Virtues and not getting waylaid by Vices and the Devil.

The soul, to Hildegard, was the animating force of a person. Placed in each person by God, it longs to keep the person healthy and whole as God created them to be. She saw the Vices as lures of Satan meant to mar God's creation. Her understanding of who we are was that all begin our lives as beloved by God. She described the relationship of the soul to the body and to God in these ways:

---

1. 'The Soul and Its Tent' Image on this page: Fol. 022 of the Rupertsberg Scivias Codex of Saint Hildegard of Bingen, around 1175, original lost since 1945, hand copy on parchment 1930, Abbey of St. Hildegard, Rüdesheim-Eibingen.
2. Dronke, Peter, editor. *Nine Medieval Latin Plays*. Cambridge University Press, 2008.

Danae Ashley, M.Div., M.A., LMFT

> *Indeed, the soul, which is a breath from God, possesses a rushing course, as too wisdom encircled the compass of heaven with a rushing course. Thus, with the seven gifts of the Holy Spirit and the five senses, a person begins and perfects all his works through the soul, as too the seventh month ripens all the earth's fruits… Indeed, the soul moves and sustains a person in his many powers with its sighs by the Holy Spirit's admonition, because it causes him in repentance to gather up all the viridity of the virtues, to scrub clean the wounds of sin. At this the soul rejoices, ever desiring to arrive at the eternal tabernacles and dwell in them without end (231, The Book of Divine Works, Part I, Vision 4).*[3]
>
> *For God created Man with all creation connected to him beneath the sun, so that he would not be alone upon the earth, just as God himself is not alone in heaven, but is glorified in all the heavenly harmonies. Moreover, all that surrounds humankind upon the earth endures with them upon the earth, until that number is fulfilled, that God established to be fulfilled (260-261, The Book of Divine Works, Part I, Vision 4).*
>
> *Indeed, as described above, the flesh lives through life, and it would not fully be flesh except through life—and so flesh is one with life, and life one with flesh. To this unity God attended when he empowered the flesh and blood in Adam by the breath that he sent into him. For God then looked upon the flesh that he would one day wear, and held it with burning love (261, The Book of Divine Works, Part I, Vision 4).*

That last line, "*For God then looked upon the flesh that he would one day wear, and held it with burning love*" is, in my opinion, one of the most meaningful statements Hildegard ever wrote. It captures the imagination of what it means to be wholly loved simply because you are a human being. Contemporary psychotherapists, especially Adler, would view this as having positive regard for the other and

---

3. Hildegard of Bingen. *The Book of Divine Works*. Translated by Nathaniel M. Campbell. Washington, DC: The Catholic University of America Press, 2021.

oneself—to be worthy of love just by existing. And again, Hildegard exemplifies the importance of holism—body and soul cannot be severed from one another:

> *Indeed, the Word is clothed with flesh such that Word and flesh are one—yet not such that one is transformed into the other, but rather that they are one in the unity of person. But the body is also the garment of the soul, and the soul functions by working with the flesh. Yet the body would be nothing without the soul, and the soul could do nothing without the body. So they are one in Man and are Man; and thus the work of God—Man—was made in God's image and likeness* (261, The Book of Divine Works, Part I, Vision 4)

In a simplistic way, the Virtues were prescriptions for a general healthy lifestyle (fruits of the Spirit as a result) and the Vices were diseases that would create mental, physical, and spiritual unrest. We will explore these in more detail later in the chapter. As progressive as we see Hildegard through our contemporary lens, she was very much a product of her time and this worldview of the Devil being around every corner is consistent with medieval theology.

"For God then looked upon the flesh that he would one day wear, and held it with burning love."

What do I imagine it feels like to be loved this way? If I believed I was loved like this, would it change anything?

We also cannot discount Hildegard's approach to healing as one being steeped in Benedictine life. The framework and interplay of liturgy, music, work, and prayer are woven throughout Hildegard's own recipes for healing. For an excellent deep dive into this topic, see Margot E. Fassler's *Cosmology and the Liturgy*.[4]

---

4. Fassler, Margot E. *Cosmos, Liturgy, and the Arts in the Twelfth Century: Hildegard's Illuminated "Scivias."* Philadelphia (Penn.): University of Pennsylvania Press, 2022, 242.

This worldview also brings into play the dichotomy of spirit vs. flesh, which was the prevalent understanding of the relationship between humanity and God at the time. Hildegard distinctively brings this separation back together in her visions, again focusing on wholeness:

> Yet the soul is not flesh and blood, but rather fills them up, so that it causes them to be alive with itself—for the rational soul has its origins from God, who breathed life into the first form. Thus soul and flesh exist as a single work in two natures. But the soul introduces into the human body air for thinking, heat for concentrating, fire for sustaining, water for ingrafting, and viridity for flourishing, just as the body was made in its original foundation. Above and below, around and within the body—the soul is everywhere. And this is the way of human existence (*The Book of Divine Works*, Part I, Vision 4).[5]

The Soul is also everywhere endangered by the snares of the Devil. These are seen in the many Vices that a person could be lured into. The only way to combat them was to turn to God and practice their opposite Virtues.

Virtues

The Virtues were not angelic beings, but the spiritual ideals specifically linked to what we in our contemporary time call mental health. The Virtues bring about the fruits of the spirit found listed in Scripture: love, joy, peace, patience, kindness, generosity, faithfulness, gentleness, and self-control (Galatians 5:22-23).

In 1150, after being stricken with illness for not following God's vision of moving her nuns from Disibodenberg to found the Rupertsberg monastery near Bingen, Hildegard and 20 nuns were

---

5. Hildegard of Bingen. *The Book of Divine Works*. Translated by Nathaniel M. Campbell. Washington, DC: The Catholic University of America Press, 2021.

able to leave with Abbot Kuno's reluctant acquiescence. Her illness was precipitated by the abbot's unwillingness to release them, even after Archbishop Henry I of Mainz stepped in and gave his permission.

In 1152, as they were waiting for the Rupertsberg monastery to be completed, Hildegard wrote a medieval morality play or sacred drama, one of the earliest we have record of in Europe, called *Ordo Virtutum*, perhaps for the new building's dedication. In this cosmic drama, the human Soul, or Anima as she is called in the play, is subjected to the Devil wandering around, shouting and snarling questions at her, and trying to bring her to harm. Anima "does not fall victim to specific vices but rather fails to comprehend the power inherent in her virginal nature; that is, she does not recognize that the body in which she is clothed was created by God, for she does not have appropriate Knowledge of God."[6]

Several of the Virtues are from the *Rule of St. Benedict*, tying it to the monastic way of life and values,[7] while others are from *Scivias* III.iii-x. Hildegard brings together these sources to create an incarnational dramatization of what is happening in the spiritual and emotional realms.

In her vision, Hildegard even sees what they wear—white clothing and shoes, plus one who has crystal shoes—to represent their purity. *"Some of them go with white hair and bare heads, and without a cloak;* which is to say that the virtues, which are joined in pure innocence in human minds, are without a veil of evil habits, and are not surrounded by worldly leanings, but entirely flee the influence of vice" (*Scivias* III.viii).[8] Echoes of these garments will be

---

6. Davidson, Audrey Ekdahl. *The Ordo Virtutum of Hildegard of Bingen: Critical Studies*. Medieval Institute Publications, 1992. 48.
7. Fassler, Margot E. *Cosmos, Liturgy, and the Arts in the Twelfth Century: Hildegard's Illuminated "Scivias."* Philadelphia (Penn.): University of Pennsylvania Press, 2022, 165-166.
8. Hildegard of Bingen, Caroline Walker Bynum, and Barbara Newman. *Hildegard of Bingen: Scivias*. Translated by Mother Columba Hart and Jane Bishop. First Edition. New York: Paulist Press, 1990, 441.

embodied not only in the presentation of *Ordo Virtutum*, but also in Hildegard's convent on feast days.

Hildegard acknowledges how different personalities engage the work of the Virtues individually, thus affecting their overall mental health and wellbeing. *"But there are differences among these virtues; which is to say that, though they are unanimous in their desire, they work diverse works in people"* (*Scivias* III.viii).[9] The Virtue of Mercy, for instance, manifests differently in my work as a psychotherapist than it does for a judge or a postal worker or a school teacher. While we may each be like the Good Samaritan and help someone on the side of the road, the way we would exercise mercy in the role we play in our work is unique, based on the power we have and our own temperament. From a psychotherapy standpoint, Hildegard is affirming once again God's "truth through personality"[10]—we cannot be someone else; we can only be uniquely ourselves.

The Virtues guide us back to concord with the Living Light. This is a brief list with a simple key to where each is found. You can see where they overlapped and note that they are not all listed here. Additional Virtues are found in *Scivias* III.iii-x:[11]

---

9. Ibid., 442.
10. Phillips Brooks, 19th century Episcopal priest and renowned preacher.
11. Fassler, Margot E. *Cosmos, Liturgy, and the Arts in the Twelfth Century: Hildegard's Illuminated "Scivias."* Philadelphia (Penn.): University of Pennsylvania Press, 2022, 190.

My Sap is Rising

Virtues

Galatians 5:22-23

Love, Joy, Peace, Patience, Kindness, Generosity, Faithfulness, Gentleness, Self-control

Edifice of Salvation (Scivias III.iii)

Knowledge of God
Humility
Victory

Ordo Virtutum

Knowledge of God
Humility
Charity
Fear of the Lord
Obedience
Faith
Hope
Chastity
Innocence
Contempt of the World
Love of Heaven
Discipline
Modesty
Mercy
Victory
Discernment
Patience

Rule of St. Benedict

Humility
Charity
Fear of the Lord
Obedience
Faith
Hope
Chastity
Innocence
Discipline
Modesty
Mercy
Patience

Vices

Galatians 5:19-21

Fornication
Impurity
Licentiousness
Idolatry
Sorcery
Emnity
Strife
Jealousy
Anger
Quarrels
Dissentions
Factions
Envy
Drunkenness
Carousing
...and other such things.

Liber Vitae Meritorum

Love of the World
Petulance
Diversion
Hardness of Heart
Laziness
Foolish Joy
Gluttony
Severeness
Impiety
Falsehood
Desire for Contention
Unhappiness
Immoderation
Hex
Worldly Desire
Discordia
Fatuity
Frivolity
Avarice
Concern for Earthly Things
Obstination
Perdition of Souls
Pride
Envy
Conceit
Disobedience
Incredulity
Despair
Lust
Injustice
Forgetting God
Inconstancy
Sadness of Living in the World

Danae Ashley, M.Div., M.A., LMFT

Fassler asserts:

> Hildegard's virtues are seats of wisdom; they are 'incarnating.' The women reenacting the play *Ordo Virtutum* did so with their knowledge of the treatise providing an exegetical understanding of what they were doing and why. The play, in the context of *Scivias*, represents the procreative power of their actions as nuns. They are models for the defeating of evil, both in the monastery and in the world at large, and Satan wants them to fail...It is the prophetic understanding of Incarnational power that lies at the heart of Anima's regaining of spiritual health, represented by what she is able to sing.[12]

While Hildegard's focus was on the spiritual nature of the Virtues, there is certainly psychological impact. Many of the Virtues have strong social interest motivations and outcomes. For example, there have been contemporary studies about the correlation between charity (generosity) and happiness in life. People who give of their time and/or money to others tend to have a greater sense of well-being which translates to happiness.[13] [14] [15] One of my professors at Adler Graduate School once told the story of Adler's approach to mild situational depression: the depressed person should make their neighbor a cup of tea. Social interest is one of Adler's foundational tenets and one solution for this type of mental

---

12. Fassler, Margot E. *Cosmos, Liturgy, and the Arts in the Twelfth Century: Hildegard's Illuminated "Scivias."* Philadelphia (Penn.): University of Pennsylvania Press, 2022,, 195.
13. Park, Soyoung Q., et al. "A Neural Link between Generosity and Happiness." *Nature Communications*, vol. 8, no. 1, July 2017, 15964. www.nature.com, https://doi.org/10.1038/ncomms15964.
14. *Measuring Happiness in the Social Sciences: An Overview.* https://doi.org/10.1177/1440783321991655. Accessed 14 Mar. 2025.
15. Utah State University. *Does Giving Make You Happier? Or Do Happier People Give? - Discovery Fall 2017 - Science.* https://www.usu.edu/science/discovery/fall-2017/does-giving-make-you-happy. Accessed 14 Mar. 2025.

ailment is to get out of oneself and think of another. Not only is this psychologically helpful, but it is also a spiritual practice.

From a Christian perspective, God created human beings to be in relationship with God, with each other, with Creation, and with Self. Our bodies were not created to be separate from our minds and souls. When we engage the Virtues, we are moving toward one of those relationships and connection, especially with God.

When Virtues are embodied, the psyche and the soul benefit. Remember the compassionate cup of tea from the Holiday Inn Express front desk clerk? It certainly lifted my spirits to receive it, and I think it did his, too.

Vices

"Now the works of the flesh are obvious: sexual immorality, impurity, debauchery, idolatry, sorcery, enmities, strife, jealousy, anger, quarrels, dissensions, factions, envy, drunkenness, carousing, and things like these. I am warning you, as I warned you before: those who do such things will not inherit the kingdom of God" (Galatians 5:20-21).

The Vices from the *Liber Vitae Meritorum* (The Book of the Rewards of Life) are listed in the chart on page 71. As you can see, there are many to avoid. We cannot truly comprehend from our position in contemporary modern life how serious these Vices were to medieval people, especially religiously pious ones. Some of the Vices revealed your character, others proved your status in society, and all of them drew you away from God. Today we struggle with the same Vices, perhaps named differently. Human nature does not change.

As part of my *Hildegard and Psychotherapy* workshops, I facilitate an exercise based on one Dr. Annette Esser taught us at the 2024 Hildegard conference. I have created laminated cards of heavy stock paper that have Vices on one side and Virtues on the other. I place them around the room and have people choose a Vice that they feel like they struggle with and stand by it. Eventually, there are small groups of people standing by their Vice and I encourage them to discuss why they chose it and how they struggle with it. It is a vulnerable thing to share with strangers, and yet it is healing.

After about five minutes of discussion, I have them flip the card over to see the Virtue that corresponds with the Vice. I then invite them to discuss at least one concrete way that they can move toward God by employing their Virtue. It is always fascinating to watch people's body language change from when they are finding and talking about their Vice (hesitant, often closed) to talking about their Virtue (more confident, open posture). This exercise always ends in connection, and people say that it is one of their favorite parts of the workshop.

Virtues draw us toward others. Vices do not. I witness this embodiment every time I lead this exercise. Vices slink down back alleys at night and spend the days using our energy to keep the secret. What does secrecy often do? According to Brené Brown, it brings its friend, shame, with it. "Shame needs three things to grow out of control in our lives: secrecy, silence, and judgment."[16] Vices bring those three things in spades.

At face value, it would seem like Vices are operating as their own agents, that they are unrelated to their opposite Virtue. Instead, the Vice is a distortion that is intertwined with the Virtue it is seeking to draw you away from—ultimately drawing you away from God. In Hildegard's worldview, we are already sinful creatures because of the Fall of Adam and Eve in the Garden of Eden. Since then, our world is not as it should be—it is distorted—and sin is in everyone.

The 'S' Word

Let's pause here and talk briefly about sin, as it is a loaded word in contemporary life. The idea of 'sin' as "the seeking of our own will

---

16. Brown, Brené. *The Gifts of Imperfection: 10th Anniversary Edition: Features a New Foreword and Brand-New Tools*. Anniversary edition, Hazelden Publishing, 2022.

instead of the will of God, thus distorting our relationship with God, with other people and with all creation"[17] in current Anglican/Episcopal Church theology (my background) concurs with Hildegard in the interrelatedness of all things and within a person (mind, body, spirit). Any time there is sin—which psychologically we may name as behaviors such as being self-serving, cruel, manipulative, thinking only of oneself, having no respect for self or others, etc. and have pathologized under names like Narcissistic Personality Disorder, Conduct Disorder, Antisocial Personality Disorder, etc.—there is distortion and damage to our interconnection to God, Creation, others, and ourselves. This also includes hurt and trauma we have inflicted on others because of our own hurt and trauma for which we have not sought healing. Pain that is not transformed continues to be transmitted.

Vices are sin's distortion of good things acted out. In Hildegard's work *Liber Vitae Meritorium* (*The Book of the Rewards of Life*), her visions include Vices of the world and the response of the Virtues. For example, she says of Gluttony:

And behold, just as I had seen various other sins in this cloud, I now saw eight other sins in various images in a similar manner. I saw a certain image, like a serpent, lying on its back in the darkness I mentioned earlier...

*...**The Words of Gluttony** This image said: "God created all things. How then can I be spoiled by all these things? If God did not think these things were necessary, he would not have made them. Therefore, I would be a fool if I did not want these things, especially since God does not want man's flesh to fail."*

The Response of Abstinence *Again I heard a voice responding to these words from the cloud that reached from the South to the West. It said: "No one should play a lyre in such a way that its strings are damaged. If its strings have been damaged,*

---

17. Church Publishing Incorporated. *Book of Common Prayer, Pew, Red*. Pew edition, Church Publishing, 1979, 848.

what sound will it make? None. You, gluttony, fill your belly so much that all your veins are bloated and are turned into a frenzy. Where then is the sweet sound of wisdom that God gave man? I [Abstinence] am, therefore, like a soft rain so that man does not have to sprout weeds. I draw moderation out of men so that their flesh does not revolt and burst, having been flooded with more life-giving food than it needs...But I encourage moderation in food so that a person is neither hungry nor too full. Thereupon I sound praises with my lyre and sing accompanied with my musical instruments. O all you faithful, restrain yourselves from gluttony. The belly of the ancient serpent gulped many things down from Eve, and it vomited forth many filthy things through Eve.[18]

Psychologically, there are a variety of reasons why a person may distort the gift of food or any other excess and follow the Vice of Gluttony. The most likely causes would be a trauma response or an underlying medical condition. With our bodies, minds, and souls being intertwined, if we begin to improve one aspect, there is a ripple effect with the others. If someone begins treatment for their trauma, they slowly find better ways to cope than stuffing their feelings down with food. They may start paying attention to when they are eating and how full they are, connecting with the why of eating—Am I hungry? Sad? Bored? Scared? They may begin to reframe how they understand their relationship with food—nurturing the body instead of using it as a protective coping mechanism. The goal is increasing self-awareness and, in turn, beginning the tender path of healing.

Adlerian Link

When I was growing up, I was very close to my maternal grandmother, my Nana. I used to watch old movies with her, and she

---

[18]. Hildegard of Bingen, and Bruce W. Hozeski. *The Book of the Rewards of Life: Liber Vitae Meritorum*. Oxford University Press, 1997, 74-75.

would talk about the glamorous movie stars of her youth. One of my favorite movies we watched was based on Oscar Wilde's novel, *The Picture of Dorian Gray,* and featured one of my favorite actresses, the young Angela Lansbury. If you are not familiar with the story, a young man makes a deal with the Devil so that he will stay young forever while his portrait ages and fades. He goes on to live a hedonistic life in pursuit of beauty and indulging in vice, not caring who he hurts along the way.

Meanwhile, his portrait gets more and more grotesque with each cruel and vice-filled act that he executes. When they reveal it at the end, it is not even recognizable as a portrait of Dorian, but a monster, as that is what his soul has become in living his chosen life.

Are there misshapen and maladaptive "monsters" inside me? What would it be like to find out where they come from and bring them from the shadows to the light?

I think Hildegard would not be surprised if she were to watch this movie. It is a powerful physical depiction of what following our own self-interest does to our soul, psyche, and body.

Adler's use of observing perceived dangers and defensive patterns can be comparable to Vice—why we do things that aren't good for us and have outgrown their helpfulness or become maladaptive. These patterns can be healed through understanding one's style of life and building on strengths and encouragement, which requires connection with others.[19] The body and the mind are united with the soul betwixt them and we cannot separate each as Dorian Gray did. As Adler wrote, "It is always necessary to look for these reciprocal actions of the mind on the body, and of the body on the mind, for both of them are parts of the whole with which we are concerned."[20]

---

19. Mariacci and Mosak, op. cit., 108.
20. Ansbacher, Heinz L., and Rowena R. Ansbacher, editors. *The Individual*

Adler also theorized that each person grows up with a sense of inferiority and tries to compensate by their unique superiority and striving for significance. He called it moving from a felt minus to a perceived plus. If maladjusted, this moves the person toward the socially useless side of life instead of the socially useful side of life. Like the Vices and Virtues, a person can choose to move toward connection or away.

The enacting of each Virtue is similar to what Adlerians would call "Acting As If"—a technique to try on a new, healthy behavior or a different way of looking at an issue. These 'virtues' are being incarnated, just as Hildegard's Virtues are in her play *Ordo Virtutum*. Adler would say 'watch the movement'—how the behavior is incarnated. People can say anything, but what do they do? These virtues and vices also point to a person's internal struggle when trying to change a behavior and move toward a positive, healing way of being.

Hildegard's incarnational way of envisioning the Virtues and Vices can be helpful to those who find healing from modalities such as Internal Family Systems (IFS), active imagination, family constellation work, and drama therapy. Putting a face or other humanizing attribute on the Vice or Virtue helps us engage with these parts of our psyche and allows us to integrate them instead of shunning them to the dark where they can overtake us in unexpected moments.

In modern day psychotherapy, Virtues can also be seen as core values, and being in alignment with one's core values assists a client in realizing their hopes and goals.

Seeking Virtues in Core Values

When I began to tell people that I was traveling to the Rhine Valley to follow Hildegard's Pilgrimage Way, they had many questions.

Psychology of Alfred Adler: A Systematic Presentation in Selections from His Writings. Harper Perennial, 1964, 225.

Why Hildegard? Why a pilgrimage? What do you hope to get from your time? Who are you going with? You're going alone? All good questions that I had good answers for, but I had deeper questions for myself. I needed to find out who I was without the identity of being a parish priest. I wanted to know what God wanted from me now that I was no longer giving energy to a parish. What would I do with the time I used to dedicate 'to the church? Ultimately, I needed to do some healing but did not know how that would take place.

One thing I did know was that I wanted to keep my private practice part-time because I have always known that I was not a person who could sit and take on people's pain eight hours a day, 4-5 days a week. I loved the creative side of parish life—teaching, preaching, leading small groups, and collaborating with people—so I knew I wanted to keep doing things like that. I was glad to have something clear as I navigated through the fog of grief in that liminal time. However, I needed something more to anchor me. I needed to focus on the virtues of a faithful life and not the vices that I could fall prey to in my hurt and deep disappointment in the Church. I needed to re-evaluate my core values for the next season of life.

Core values have long been prized in institutions and organizations for empowering a diverse set of people to gather around a shared set of values that they believe in and can work toward. Researchers Harald Askeland, Gry Espedal, Beate Jelstad Løvaas, and Stephen Sirris assert that "[v]alues are intractably connected to norms and morals: they signify worth, preferences and priorities and separate the desirable from the undesirable."[21] Any of Hildegard's Virtues could be used as a core value to help a person discern when they are sliding into Vice territory. Core values are modern psychological wayfinders in the midst of the fog of uncer-

---

21. Askeland, Harald, et al. *Understanding Values Work: Institutional Perspectives in Organizations and Leadership*. Springer International Publishing AG, 2020. *ProQuest Ebook Central*, http://ebookcentral.proquest.com/lib/csbsju/detail.action?docID=6112021. 3.

tainty. While not having the same spiritual impetus as Virtues, they operate in a similar fashion for anyone, spiritual or not, trying to live a life that is authentic and connecting. When life is stormy, they shine like beacons in the dark so you can keep moving forward in the right direction.

If you have never done core value work, there are many samples on the internet that are useful to reflect on, and I highly recommend it. While I was preparing for the pilgrimage, I did several core values worksheets that I use with my clients, and I prayed for guidance. I wanted to filter all my decisions for what to do with the time I had been given back in my week through my core values. By the time I found my first tableau about Vices and Virtues on the Pilgrimage Way, my new core values were established. I wanted to use my newfound free time doing projects that were: creative, collaborative, well-paying, and where I would get to wear beautiful clothes.[22] I cannot tell you how helpful this clarity has been in helping to shape a life that is in alignment with who God has created me to be and what I need in my current circumstances. Being a feather on the breath of God means that we must let go of what was and know that we are being supported as we fly into new winds.

---

22. I am serious about the beautiful clothes. They do not have to be expensive, but they do have to make me feel like I am my best self. And they must be colorful, usually with some sort of delicious texture and small details to make it unique.

Pilgrim's Reflection

1. Incarnating Our Virtues and Vices

- Choose three virtues that you value and three vices that you struggle with from the list below.
- With your non-dominant hand, draw or make marks on a page that represents each one.
- Look at what you put down on the page. What do you notice about this "incarnation" of these things? What is it like to see them on paper?
- Reflect on how you would like to engage them in the coming months. What can you commit to that brings in more connection with the virtues and less with the vices?

Here is a list of the Vices and their corresponding Virtues from the *Liber Vitae Meritorum*. You may have to look up what some of the words/phrases meant in medieval times to gain better understanding:

- Love of the World - Love of God
- Petulance - Discipline
- Diversion/Vanity - Modesty
- Hardness of Heart - Mercy
- Laziness/Numbness – Commitment
- Foolish Joy - God's Desire
- Gluttony - Abstinence
- Asperity - Authentic Generosity
- Impiety - Piety
- Falsehood - Truth
- Desire for Contention - Peace
- Unhappiness - Happiness
- Immoderation - Discretion
- Perdition of Souls - Salvation of Souls
- Pride - Humility

- Envy - Charity
- Conceit - Fear of God
- Disobedience - Obedience
- Incredulity- Faith
- Despair - Hope
- Lust – Chastity
- Injustice - Justice
- Anxiety (Heartburn) - Strength
- Forgetting God - Holiness
- Inconstancy - Constancy.
- Concern for earthly things - Heavenly Desire
- Obstination - Repentance
- Worldly Desire - Contempt of the World
- Discordia – Concordia
- Fatuity - Respect
- Frivolity – Sage/Stability
- Hex - True Worship of God
- Avarice - Total Detachment
- Sadness of Living in the World - Heavenly Joy

2. What is a behavior that you would like to try to change? Choose something small and obtainable and 'Act As If' you behave in the new way. After a few weeks, reflect on how it feels and if anything else needs to change to make it a permanent behavior.

3. Research Core Value assessments online and choose two to complete. How do the answers align with the Virtues you have chosen to pursue?

Benediction

This hymn is a reminder of God's fierce love for humanity. To Hildegard's hierarchical worldview, human beings are the culmination of all creation as we are made in God's image.

Group option: Have different people lead the first two sentences and all read the last sentence together.

O How Miraculous[23]

First voice
O how miraculous is
the foresight of the divine heart,
that foretold every creature.

Second voice
For when God gazed
upon the face of the human being he had formed
he saw the entirety of all his works
in that same human form.

Together
O how miraculous is the breath
that awakened humankind to life.

Symphonia (Songs) 3

---

23. Kujawa-Holbrook, Sheryl A., translator. *Hildegard of Bingen: Essential Writings and Chants of a Christian Mystic—Annotated & Explained.* 1st edition, SkyLight Paths, 2016, 101.

Chapter 4
The Four Temperaments of Personality

When I realized that I wanted to do the Hildegard of Bingen Pilgrimage Way, my organizational mind went into overdrive. I would not rest until I had my plane tickets, accommodations, what I was going to bring with me, who I was going to connect with, and how I was going to do it all in the allotted time I had. I felt tense until each detail was in place and the timeline was set.

I had never really been interested in visiting Germany and when the dates were confirmed and the tickets were bought, I immediately contacted my German friend, Simone, whom I had met when we were both foreign exchange students at the University of Aberdeen in Scotland in 1998. I decided that after 25 years, I did not care where she lived, I would find a way to see her. Luckily, Simone only lived a few hours from the Rhine Valley and so we decided that I would visit the only weekend I would be there. This meant that I would start at the end of the Pilgrimage Way—in Rüdesheim am Rhein—and take three trains to get to Simone.

This plan filled me with nervousness. While I have taken public transportation in various cities in the U.S., U.K., and France, I either knew the language or had someone with me who did. Here, I did

Danae Ashley, M.Div., M.A., LMFT

not know the language or how their train system worked. Simone also told me that sometimes the workers would go on strike, but in good German fashion, they would politely give everyone enough lead time to figure out alternatives. My nerves went up another degree with this information. When I get lost, I usually get overwhelmed and before I can figure out a logical solution, I must have a good cry (closing the stress cycle loop with a physical release—the wisdom of the body![1]). I did not want to be known as 'The American Who Cries on German Train Platforms.'

So, you can imagine the immense relief that flooded me when I received an email from Simone with the subject line "Itinerary details for help with trains" and a document attached called "Danae's Adventure." Simone understands my planner's heart. I do not know if it is because that is just the German way (to plan and be precise) or her personality, but I suspect it is a combination of both. Not only did she talk me off my ledge, but she gave me a document with screenshots of the app I needed and highlighted in the screenshots which train route I should take and which tickets I should buy. I immediately downloaded the app and got down to business. When the time came to execute the plan, I was still nervous, but much less so. Thanks to my good friend Simone and her similar personality style for planning, I was able to be an anonymous traveler and not 'The American Who Cries on German Train Platforms.'

Who Doesn't Love a Personality Test?

From the description of my personality in the situation above, what do you think my personality typology is? Would you use the Myers-Briggs Type Indicator? The Five-Factor Model of Personality? The Enneagram? Sun Sign in Astrology?

From the 5th century BCE Greeks to Hildegard and the four

---

1. See Emily Nagoski and Amelia Nagoski's book *Burnout: The Secret to Unlocking the Stress Cycle*. Random House Publishing Group. 2020.

temperaments to 18th century phrenology to 1980s teen magazine quizzes like 'What Kind of Kisser Are You?' to TikTok and Instagram reels and memes of 'What's My Lord of the Rings Character?', human beings want to know who we are. We also want to know who other people are because liking or hating a person is so much easier if we know he's a Leo Sun Sign, she's an Enneagram 8, or they are Gimli the Dwarf. Once we know a person's typology, we know the whole person, right? Well, not really.

Hildegard uses the classical notion of the four temperaments as just one piece of understanding a person and what they might need in their healing. This was a common practice stretching back centuries to the Greek philosopher and physician Hippocrates (460-370 BCE). He gave us the first personality typology using the idea that our bodies consisted of the four fluids: blood, yellow bile, black bile, and phlegm. He posited that our temperaments were influenced by the prominence of one of the four fluids over the other:

- Blood: Sanguine – pleasure-seeking and sociable
- Yellow Bile: Choleric – ambitious and extraverted
- Black Bile: Melancholic – analytical and detail-oriented
- Phlegm: Phlegmatic – relaxed and easy-going[2]

These ideas were held and enhanced by the second century physician, Galen, whose work held sway well into the fifteenth century.[3] The large, thriving Benedictine monastery of Disibodenberg would almost certainly have had a copy of Galen's work in their library so that they could heal people in the infirmary as well as study medicine. Hildegard may have had access to this

---

2. These descriptions are found in many places. Here is one article from the Johns Hopkins Newsletter: "New Study Reveals Four Major Personality Types." *The Johns Hopkins News-Letter*, https://www.jhunewsletter.com/article/2018/10/new-study-reveals-four-major-personality-types. Accessed 15 Mar. 2025.
3. Retief, F. P., and L. Cilliers. "The Influence of Christianity on Graeco-Roman Medicine Up to the Renaissance." *Akroterion*, vol. 46, 2001. akroterion.journals.ac.za, https://doi.org/10.7445/46-0-120. 63.

or to someone who could teach her the common recipes and cures for healing to care for her own community, especially after she was elected *magistra*[4] following Jutta's death in 1136. She never mentions any works that she learned from except the Bible, so it is difficult to determine how she learned about the four humors.

Hildegard believed that the humors had to keep balanced in the body, just like the four elements (earth, air, water, and fire) to maintain health.[5] You can get an idea of her worldview from this section of her *Causes and Cures*[6]:

> *God made the elements of the world and, just as the human being exists in the elements, these elements are in the human and the human works with them. The elements, fire, air, water, and earth, are entangled and conjoined with each other. One cannot be separated from another, and they hold themselves together and are called the firmament.*
>
> *If a human were to live as appointed, all the seasons, and breezes in their seasons, would behave equitably: this spring would be as last spring, this summer as last, etc. When a person pays no attention to the fear or love of God, all the elements and seasons exceed their ordained places, as happens in a person's inner organs when a person exceeds moderation. When he oversteps justice with his ill deeds, he aggravates and darkens the sun and the moon; accordingly, they create storms, rain, and drought (ii).*

Hildegard develops her own conceptualization of the four humors

---

4. *Magistra* is the honorific title for the role of a 'spiritual teacher.' Hildegard was under the authority of Abbot Kuno and later Abbot Helengarus of the Disibodenberg and was never officially an Abbess herself, although she acted as the spiritual mother for her nuns. *FAQ*. http://www.hildegard-society.org/p/faq.html. Accessed 15 Mar. 2025.
5. Newman, Barbara, ed. Florence Eliza Glaze, "Chapter 7: Medical Writer," *Voice of the Living Light: Hildegard of Bingen and Her World*. First Edition, University of California Press, 1998. 135.
6. Throop, Priscilla. *Causes and Cures of Hildegard of Bingen*. 2nd ed., MedievalMS, 2012.ii.

with the idea of humoral balance (*eucrasia*) and imbalance (*dyscrasia*) based on her understanding of a hierarchical cosmos.[7] The higher elements are celestial and immaterial and the lower are terrestrial and material.

> Similarly, the humors within each person are divided into two classes, the dominant *flegmata* and the subordinate, occasionally obstreperous *livores*. When the humors maintain their respective dominant and subordinate relationships, the body exists in a state of health. But when the subordinate humors overcome the designated dominant ones, the body and mind of the person are adversely affected; the greater the degree of disharmony, the graver the illness that befalls the sufferer.[8]

She believed that the Fall of humanity created an alternative reality to what God intended and altered the human body so that illness, as well as sin, was introduced into life's experience.[9] "Certainly she would not have denied the efficacy of faith and prayer, but she does not advocate them as the first course of action. Instead, Hildegard privileges the practice of medicine, based on the knowledge of the powers of created things, a knowledge granted by God but deserving careful attention."[10]

---

7. For a deep and excellent exploration of the humors and elements in Hildegard's medicine, please see: Sweet, Victoria. *Rooted in the Earth, Rooted in the Sky*. 1st edition, Routledge, 2006.
8. Newman, Barbara, ed. Florence Eliza Glaze, "Chapter 7: Medical Writer," *Voice of the Living Light: Hildegard of Bingen and Her World*. First Edition, University of California Press, 1998, 135.
9. Ibid., 135.
10. Ibid., 136-137.

Danae Ashley, M.Div., M.A., LMFT

The Four Temperaments

Building on Hildegard's understanding of the spiritual foundation of humanity, it is important to understand how she would view the psyche and physiology of a person through the lens of the four humors.[11] She believed that the different physiological makeup between male and female, as well as differences within each gender, determined which roles they should play in life. Through observation, Hildegard believed that differences in physiology existed for a reason, such as the idea that the different division in a woman's skull served a specific purpose: for the skull to open and allow blood to flow out during menstruation.[12] "Consequently, the different temperaments of men and women—four for each—are determined by their physiologically different profiles, which in turn broadly influence the diverse personality traits of each as well as their health, sexuality, and longevity."[13]

Hildegard followed Plato and Galen's model of the four personality styles based on physiology and behavior: Sanguine (Artisan/eagerly optimistic), Choleric (Idealist/passionate), Melancholic (Guardian/doleful), and Phlegmatic (Rational/calm).

Like Hildegard, Adler believed that physical ailments and structure called for compensation in psychological ways. He warned against considering a person as a 'type' because "every person has an individual style of life"[14] and "must be studied in the light of his

---

11. If you are interested in taking your own assessment based on what Hildegard would have known, you can find a "for fun" personality quiz here: http://openpsychometrics.org/tests/O4TS/
12. Newman, Barbara, ed. Florence Eliza Glaze, "Chapter 7: Medical Writer," *Voice of the Living Light: Hildegard of Bingen and Her World*. First Edition, University of California Press, 1998, 83.
13. Ibid., 138-139.
14. Ansbacher, Heinz L., and Rowena R. Ansbacher, editors. *The Individual Psychology of Alfred Adler: A Systematic Presentation in Selections from His Writings*. Harper Perennial, 1964, 166.

own peculiar development."[15] These typologies should be used with caution, as Adler wrote:

> *To present the individual understandably, in words, requires an extensive reviewing of all his facets. Yet too often psychologists are tempted away from this recognition to take the easier but unfruitful roads of classification. That is a temptation to which, in practical work, we must never yield. It is for teaching purposes only, to illuminate the broad field, that we shall designate here four different types in order temporarily to classify the attitude and behavior of individuals toward outside problems.*[16]

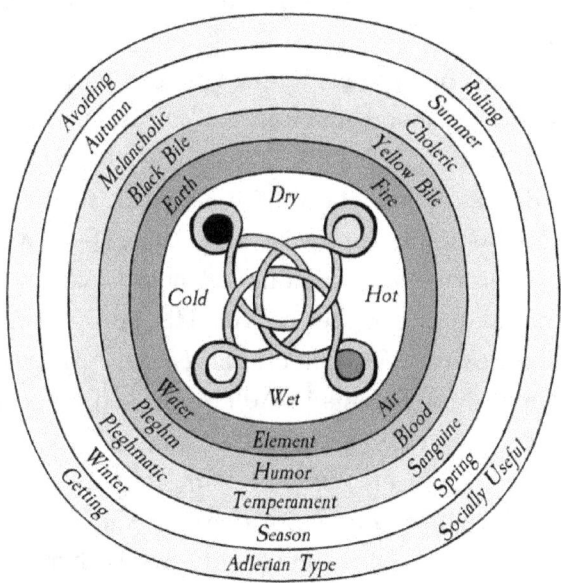

Adler focuses on a person's social interest when using typology. Adler called his classification the Social Interest-Activity Types which others have referred to as the Four Styles of Life. Several

---

15. Ibid., 167.
16. Ibid., 167.

years before Adler offered his typology, he studied the ancient Four Temperaments that Hildegard used for her own work. His conclusions related everything back to a person's social interest and I have included his temperament classification in parentheses after the Social Interest-Activity Type in the list below:[17]

- **Ruling type** (Choleric): aggressive, dominating people who don't have much social interest or cultural perception.
- **Getting type** (Phlegmatic): dependent people who take rather than give.
- **Avoiding type** (Melancholic): people who try to escape life's problems and take little part in socially constructive activity.
- **Socially Useful type** (Sanguine): people with a great deal of social interest and activity.

One of Adler's followers, Rudolph Dreikurs, further developed this idea in 1947 with his Four Mistaken Goals. Depending on their personality style, a person will pursue their mistaken goal when their self-esteem does not feel secure. His Four Mistaken Goals were *Retaliation, Service, Recognition, and Power.*[18] These have especially been helpful for parents in Adlerian-based parenting classes and workshops.

Since many people are familiar with the Myers-Briggs Type Indicator (MBTI) which is based, in part, on Carl Jung's Intuition, Thinking, Sensation, Feeling personality types, here are its four temperaments: "Artisan (SP) is likely also to be hedonic, sanguine, innovative, aesthetic, and probing"; "a Guardian (SJ) is also likely to be proprietary, melancholic, industrious, traditional, and scheduling"; "an Idealist (NF) is also likely to be ethical, inspired, doctri-

---

17. Ibid., 169.
18. Keirsey, David. *Please Understand Me II: Temperament, Character, Intelligence*. First Edition, Prometheus Nemesis Book Co, 1998, 25.

naire, hyperesthetic, and friendly"; "a Rational (NT) is also likely to be dialectical, curious, skeptical theoretical, and tough-minded."[19]

Hildegard had much to say about each type of personality and this adds another layer to the holism she provided in healing. These descriptions are from her work *Cause et Curae*. Which of the temperaments do you think Hildegard herself might have been?

---

19. Ibid., 26.

Danae Ashley, M.Div., M.A., LMFT

Choleric

Hildegard describes not just Choleric Men, but *Virile*, Choleric Men:

Certain males are virile, and have a strong, dense brain. The small exterior veins which nourish its covering are somewhat red. These men's faces are somewhat ruddy, as seen in certain red-colored paintings. Their thick, strong veins transport a burning blood of waxy color. They are thick around the chest, have strong arms, and are not very fat, since strong veins, blood, and limbs do not allow their flesh to be much fattened.[20]

The Choleric Woman receive a more detailed description:

Some women have thin flesh but large bones and moderate sized veins. They have thick, red blood, a pale-colored face, and are prudent and kind. They are shown respect by men, and are feared. They suffer in menstruation with very much blood. Their womb is strongly positioned, and they are fertile. Men love their ways, but avoid them a bit. These women do not draw men behind them, alluring them. If they are joined to husbands, they are chaste and observe wifely fidelity. With husbands, they are physically healthy, but if they lack them, they will feel pain in their body, and they will

---

20. Throop, Priscilla. *Causes and Cures of Hildegard of Bingen*. Second edition, MedievalMS, 2012, 59.

be weak, as much from not knowing to whom they might show womanly fidelity, as from the fact they do not have husbands. If the flows of the menstrual period cease before the due time, they will easily be paralytic and they will be enervated and infirm in their humors, or they will feel pain in their liver, or easily incur the black tumor of dragunculus, or their breasts swell up from cancer.[21]

Let us pause here and notice what Hildegard is observing. In men: Virility, the brain, the veins, the color of the vein covering, their face color, the thickness of their chest, strong arms, and lack of fat. In women, she goes into greater detail: the thickness of their flesh, bone size, vein size, the color of their face, the color of their blood, their disposition (prudent and kind), how they are seen by men (respected and feared), what their menstruation is like, where their womb is placed, their fertility, how they behave with the opposite sex, what they feel if they do not have a husband (pain and weakness), what happens when menstruation ceases (become paralytic, infirm in their humors or feel pain in their liver, or incur the black tumor, breasts swell up from cancer).

That is a lot of observation with much implication in the overall picture of mental health. Hildegard gives keen observations in each of those sections of the body for each temperament. She would need to be sensitive to what might ail a person with this personality profile and cause them distress even before they suffered so it could be prevented.

If a person were normally Choleric and were being visited by a spell of imbalance of humor, it would be important for Hildegard to understand what she would be trying to balance them back to. While each person is an individual, using the temperaments is a type of shortcut to understanding what is needed for healing.

---

21. Ibid., 73.

Danae Ashley, M.Div., M.A., LMFT

Melancholic

Here are Hildegard's observations of Melancholic Men:

There are other men whose brain is fatty, and the covering of the brain and its veins are disordered. They have a somber colored face, so that their eyes are somewhat fiery and snake-like. They have strong, hard veins which contain black, thick blood. They have thick, hard flesh and thick bones, which hold little marrow. This, however, burns so strongly that they are incontinent with women, just like animals and snakes. The wind in their loins has three qualities: fiery, windy, and mixed with the vapor of melancholy. They have the correct love toward nothing. Bitter, greedy, and foolish, they are excessive in lust. Lacking moderation with women, they are like donkeys. If, at some time, they cease from this lust, they easily incur mental illness, so they will be madmen. When they exercise this lust in conquering women, they do not suffer insanity; however, the embrace, which they ought to have in soberness toward women, is twisted, hateful, and deadly, as if of violent wolves. Some of these men, because of their strong veins and their strongly burning marrow, are with women willingly, in accord with human nature; nevertheless they hate them. Some are able to avoid the feminine sex, because they do not love women nor wish to have them, but in their hearts they are as fierce as lions and have the character of bears. Nevertheless, they are useful and prudent in the work of their hands, and willingly work. The wind of delecta-

tion falling into the testicles of melancholic men, comes with great lack of restraint and sudden onset; just like a wind which suddenly and forcefully moves an entire house. This wind stimulates the penis with such great tyranny that, when it ought to blossom into flower, it twists itself in cruel, snakelike behavior and holds malice, just as the progeny of a deadly, murderous viper. Diabolical suggestion so rages in these men that, if they could, they would kill a woman in intimate connection. In them are no deeds of loving kindness or devotion.

Sons and daughters which they bring forth often have diabolical madness in their vices and character, since they were sent forth without love..."[22]

And of the Melancholic Woman:

Other women have meager flesh, large veins, moderate sized bones, blood more blue than red, and a face as if mixed with a bluish-black color. They are fickle and vague in their thoughts and weary, wasting away in distress. They are enervated by nature, so that sometimes they are vexed by melancholy. They suffer very much blood in their menstrual period, and are sterile, since they have a weak, fragile womb. Whence they are not able to receive, retain, or warm the man's semen. They are healthier, stronger, and happier without husbands than with them since, if they are with husbands, they are enfeebled. Men turn away from them and flee them because they do not address men affably, and they love men very little. If these women at any time have delectation of the flesh, it quickly ceases.

Certain melancholic women, if they are with robust, sanguine husbands, sometimes, having reached the strong age of fifty, bear at least one child. With a weak-natured husband, they do not conceive, but remain sterile. If menstruation ceases before due time

---

22. Throop, Priscilla. *Causes and Cures of Hildegard of Bingen.* Second edition, MedievalMS, 2012, 61-62.

> *according to the nature of woman, they sometimes will have gout or swollen legs, or they incur mental illness which rouses melancholy, or pain of the back and kidneys, or their body quickly swells up, since the lymph and foulness, which ought to be purged through menstruation, remains lodged in them. If they are not aided in their infirmity, and not liberated from it, either by the help of God or through medicine, they will quickly die.*[23]

In these descriptions, we get a little more about the male sexual characteristics and their disposition, as well as observations about their offspring. Hildegard's observations suggest that melancholic women might make the best nuns. I also think she is talking about menopause when she mentions the cessation of menstruation. Once these women cease menstruating, their bodies develop various ailments, including mental illness. There is currently much more research happening around perimenopause and menopause and the effects of lack of estrogen on every organ, including the brain.

As they lose estrogen, progesterone, and testosterone, many women have heightened anxiety, brain fog, and depression in addition to other diseases.[24] Although Hildegard was obviously unaware of modern research in this field, her observations are astute.

---

23. Ibid., 73-74.
24. Haver, Mary Claire. *The New Menopause: Navigating Your Path Through Hormonal Change with Purpose, Power, and Facts.* Rodale Books, 2024. Note: I highly recommend following Dr. Haver's social media and website for excellent, well-researched, relevant information on this season of a woman's life. I also recommend menopause.org for information and to find a menopause certified practitioner in your area in the United States.

Phlegmatic

The following are Hildegard's observations of Phlegmatic Men:

Other men have a fatty, white, and dry brain. Even the small veins of that brain are more white than red. They have large, murky eyes and a womanish-colored face. Their skin is not bright, but is of an almost dead color. They have wide, soft veins which contain little blood, which is not blood-like, but foamy. Their body flesh is sufficient, but soft like that of women. They have strong limbs, but lack a daring, keen mind. In their thinking and conversation, they are bold and keen, like a fire whose flame suddenly rises, then falls. In their dress they show daring, but have none in their deeds. Their conversation shows opinion rather than action. The wind in their loins has a small amount of fire, so that it is slightly warm, like water which is barely warm. The testicles, which ought to be like two bellows for rousing a fire, do not contain a plentitude of fire. They are derelict in weakness and have no strength to cause an erection. Because they are able to cohabit with both men and women, and because they are loyal, these men can be loved in intimate embrace. They do not hold deadly hatred, but because in their bodies they have an inkling of the original creation, where Adam and Eve came forth without carnal embrace, they are lacking in reproductive power. Since their semen is not like other men's, they are unable to be virile, either in their beard or in other manly attributes. They are not envious, and because of their reputation of

> being naturally weak, they love women who are also weak, because a woman in her weakness is like a child. Thence they sometimes begin to warm up a bit, and grow a trace of a beard, like earth which brings forth a small amount of grass. These men do not have the perfection of a plow in cleaving the earth, because, being sterile, they are unable to unite with women like fertile men. Even in their mind, they are not much troubled with lust, except sometimes they consider the idea or option. Having this weakness in their bodies, they are slow in mental powers. Their veins are fragile, like reeds and certain herbs; those in their temples are not full of vital force. These men are not called virile since their veins are cold and their semen is weak and unripe, like foam, and they cannot hold it back for the proper amount of time.[25]

On the Phlegmatic Woman:

> There are other women whose flesh does not increase much because they have large veins. Their blood is somewhat healthy, but white because it contains a bit of poison, whence it receives its white color. They have a stern face of swarthy complexion. Vigorous, useful, with a somewhat virile mind, they sustain neither too small nor too great, but moderately flowing, streams of blood in their menstrual period. Since they have large veins, they are very fecund for offspring and easily conceive. Their womb and all the internal organs are strongly positioned. They attract men and lead them behind them, and men love them. If they wish to keep themselves from men, they are able to refrain from joining with them, which debilitates them a little, but not much. If they avoid joining with men, they become hard to deal with and serious in their behavior; if they are with men, and refuse to hold themselves back from union, they become incontinent and overflow with lust, just like men. Since they are a bit virile, because of the life force in them, they

---

25. Throop, Priscilla. *Causes and Cures of Hildegard of Bingen*. 2nd ed., MedievalMS, 2012, 62-63.

sometimes grow a bit of downy hair on their chin. If they cease menstruation before the natural time, they sometimes incur the mental illness called delirium, or they will be splenetic or dropsical, or the protruding flesh which is always in ulcers grows on them, or a fleshy pustule grows on the surface of some limb, like the excrescence on a tree or piece of fruit.[26]

Once again, Hildegard's observations are keen and fascinating. I wonder if Phlegmatic men came to the monastery infirmary in search of sexual aids? The way Hildegard describes their issues, they would need what we call today sex therapy or herbal remedy for arousal, premature ejaculation, and erectile dysfunction. Of course, at that time, the woman would likely have been blamed for not being able to bear a child with a man such as this, but I am sure there would have been distress on both sides. Like many modern couples, they probably would not talk about it for similar reasons—it is private, it is about God's blessing (certainly in Hildegard's time and for some religious sects in our time), it is embarrassing in light of the culture placing high value on reproduction, and they do not know who to talk to about it or how it would be cured except through an act of Divine power.[27]

---

26. Ibid., 72-73.
27. We are fortunate to live in a time where sex therapy is available across the United States. If you are struggling in similar ways to the Phlegmatic person, I encourage you to get a physical examination from your doctor and look at the American Association of Sexuality Educators, Counselors, and Therapists (AASECT) website to find a local therapist in your area of the United States: https://www.aasect.org/

Danae Ashley, M.Div., M.A., LMFT

Sanguine

Last, but not least, we have Hildegard's observations of Sanguine Men:

Some males have a warm brain and their face is delightful color, a mixture of white and red.

Their sleek veins are filled with blood which is thick and of the correct red color. They have in them a delightful humor, oppressed by neither sadness nor bitterness, which the distress of melancholy flees and avoids.

Since they have a warm brain and correct blood, and their humors are not oppressed, their bodies have fatty flesh. The inclination for intercourse, which is in their thighs, is more windy than fiery, and consequently they are able to practice abstinence.

The great amount of wind in their things quells and tempers their fire...It is necessary for these men to join a habitation of men since their womanly nature is sweeter and more gentle than virile nature. They are able to be with women in honesty and fertility, and they are able to abstain from them...Because they are gentle in sight, sound, and thoughts, they, more often than others, emit a watery, unripe foam; this happens to them while sleeping, as well as when they are awake. And more easily than certain others, either by themselves or with other things, they are released from the heat of lust.[28]

The Sanguine Woman has the following characteristics:

Certain women are of a plump nature and have soft, agreeable flesh, thin veins, and correct blood without lymph. Since their veins are thin, they hold less blood and, more is blood mixed with their flesh, and their flesh increases more. These women have a clear, white face and are in the embrace of love. They are loveable and exacting in their skills. They are content in mind and suffer moderately flowing blood in their streams of menstruation. The vessel of their womb is strongly positioned for child-bearing, whence they are fertile and able to receive the male semen. Nevertheless they do not produce many children. If they are without husbands, and do not give birth to offspring, they easily ail in their body. If they have husbands, they are healthy. If the drops of blood of the menstrual period cease to flow before the natural time, they sometimes will be melancholic or suffer from pain in the side, or a worm grows in their flesh or protruding tumors called scrofula[29] *erupt on them, or leprosy, although moderate, grows on them.*[30]

It sounded like there must have been some Sanguine men in the Disibodenberg monastery among the various churchmen with whom Hildegard corresponded if this description is accurate. It would not be surprising. Certain personalities do have more of a proclivity to particular vocations over others. Hildegard also seems to understand that men have nocturnal emissions, although she only mentions it here. Once again, she describes in detail what

---

28. Op.cit., Throop, 60-61.
29. Scrofula is tuberculous lymphadenitis—a rare form of tuberculosis that affects the lymph nodes in the neck.
30. Throop, Priscilla. *Causes and Cures of Hildegard of Bingen.* 2nd ed., MedievalMS, 2012, 72.

happens to women when they no longer menstruate. The mental health issue of melancholia is mentioned for menopausal women. In her holistic healing, it would be vital to know where a woman was in her reproductive life cycle so that she could be properly cared for in body, mind, and spirit.

Now that we have taken a quick tour of Hildegard's way of assessing personality, take a moment to reflect: With which temperament do you think Hildegard would have identified? And what about you? Peter Dronke remarks in *Women Writers of the Middle Ages* "Hildegard, I submit, understood herself as a melancholic woman. If we juxtapose with her description of the type another key passage in *Causae et curae*...and relate these passages to all she tells us of herself in the autobiographic notes in the *Vita*, the implied diagnosis is clear."[31]

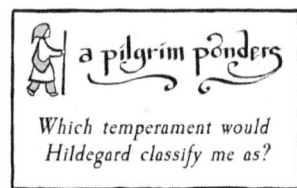

Which temperament would Hildegard classify me as?

Adlerian Link

Like Hildegard, Adler believed that physical attributes mattered to personality. He called this 'organ inferiority.' Who you are today did not start in your mind, but in the body. When we are born, we are born imperfect. Some organs are superior (stronger) or inferior (weaker) to others. Superior organs begin to compensate or over-compensate for the inferior organs. This process is mirrored in the mind. Adler was a physician who examined how the body and mind worked together and interfaced with each other and the social milieu outside themselves. He believed that we are responding to a pull to the outer world, in contrast to his contemporary, Freud, who operated from drive theory—behavior being motivated by unconscious drives such as life/death and sex/ego.

---

31. Dronke, Peter. *Women Writers of the Middle Ages: A Critical Study of Texts from Perpetua.* First Edition, Cambridge University Press, 1985, 182.

For Adler, significance embedded in social context is what we desire. Consider this example:

John, the first-born child, started crawling, walking, and reaching other physical developmental milestones early with the encouragement of his parents. As a toddler, he loved playing hide and seek. Later, he loved to run and took swimming lessons in elementary school.

Jane, the second child, is stouter and has shorter legs. She is later in crawling, walking, and reaching other developmental milestones. She spends a lot of time on her back, looks at her mobile and reaches to grab things. Her orientation is more around her hands and the movement in her hands. She learns to sit up and pick things up to move them in front of her. She has better fine motor skills and spent more time figuring out how things work and was praised for it.

Fast forward 15 years later and John is an athlete and Jane is a scholar. Who you are organically—your physical body—also assists in determining what you might become.

For Adler, inferiority feelings were perceptions of inadequacy—the different ways you felt you were less capable when you were a child. It is natural to accentuate the things we can do well, but this also means that we each develop ways in which we limit ourselves and in which we excel. These limitations and strengths are not good or bad. Adler believed the most important thing is what you do with them.

A Note on Lunar Prognostication

Hildegard also attributes certain personality characteristics to which day in the lunar cycle the person was conceived. Keep in mind that this one of the medieval ways of assessing a person and is not recommended for contemporary diagnosis. Here are a few interesting examples:

Danae Ashley, M.Div., M.A., LMFT

177b Something on conception. *Persons who are conceived when the moon carries along many downpours in rainy weather are easily attracted by water, causing them to drown. Persons who are conceived when the moon is shining in the burning heat of summer are easily attracted by fire, causing them to burn. Persons who are conceived during the dog days [hottest days of summer] are easily devoured by animals because these are the biting days. One who is conceived at the time of* loubroz *["rotting leaves"] will easily fall from trees and other heights...*[32]

180b The twentieth day after the new moon. *One who is conceived on the twentieth day after the new moon, if it is male, will be virile and evil. He will be a robber and a murderer and will enjoy it. He does not easily fall ill; once an infirmity has affected him, he will be seriously ill and will not live long. But if it is a female, she will be a* uerretheren *["betrayer"] and a* cedenseren *["gossip"]. She will be a poisoner and will gladly destroy people. She will easily become lunatic and will live long...*[33]

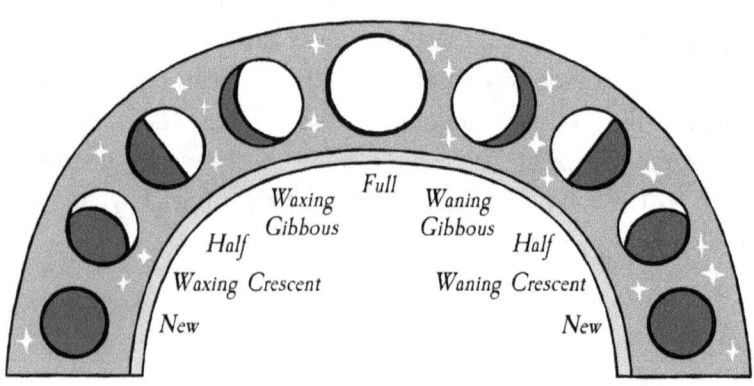

---

32. Hildegard of Bingen. *Hildegard of Bingen: On Natural Philosophy and Medicine.* Translated by Margret Berger, D. S. Brewer, 1999, 123.
33. Ibid., 124

Hildegard had many tools to work with when it came, as Adler would say, to understanding a person. I am sure these medieval personality assessments were useful to her in the convent, being the spiritual mother to a variety of personalities. In my experience of leading Episcopal congregations and other groups, I have found that using modern versions of personality assessment tools like the MTBI and Enneagram can encourage participants to develop more patience with and a greater understanding of one another.

While Adler did not write his theory on inferior feelings as theology, his idea that it is not our limitations and strengths which are good or bad, but what we do with them reminds me of Hildegard's understanding of the soul's journey. We sometimes forget that we are inherently worthy of love just by being. Hildegard believed we are God's creations in the bodies in which our souls have been placed. We have limitations and strengths, with Vices pulling us away from our Virtues, but our ultimate desire is to be transformed into who God created us to be. Each of us has a beautiful, shining soul which has been hidden through defenses and Vices along the way. It is our job to connect to it again with everything we have at our disposal.

Danae Ashley, M.Div., M.A., LMFT

Pilgrim's Reflection

1. Have you ever taken a personality or temperament assessment? If so, reflect on what you resonated with most. Has that changed over time? If not, do an internet search and find a few to try and see what you think.

2. Do you think it is helpful to categorize people using personality tests? What do we gain by categorizing ourselves and others? What do we lose?

3. Adler observed 'organ inferiority' and how a person made their way in the world because of it. Every person is striving for completeness, *not* perfection. This is what each person's trajectory looks like:

> *Striving* leads to
> > *Inferiority feelings*, which lead to
> > > *Compensation* and further *striving*.[34]

A person's *felt minus* would be how they perceived themselves as lacking and their *perceived plus* would be what they strive for to assuage the felt minus and feel superior—a more advantageous position, moving toward the final, fictional goal.

Like John and Jane in the Adlerian Link story, we all have organ inferiorities. What do you think yours are?

4. How has learning about someone else's typology helped you feel more compassion for them? Did it change the way you approached the relationship?

---

34. Maniacci and Mosak, op. cit., 32.

Benediction

Hildegard frequently talks about Wisdom in her visions and refers to Wisdom encircling everything in the journey of life, not transcending it. This portion of her hymn to the power of Wisdom reminds me of a Celtic circle prayer of protection such as St. Patrick's Breastplate.

Group option: Stand and gather in a circle. Invite three volunteers to represent the three wings. When it comes to each wing the first time the hymn is said, the volunteer enters the circle to embody its part. All three remain in the circle as you pray the hymn twice more.

O Power of Wisdom[35]

> O power of Wisdom!
> who circling, circled
> embracing all things
> in a single life-giving path.
>
> You have three wings:
> one soars to the heavens,
> the second exudes moisture from the earth,
> and the third soars everywhere.
> All praise be to you, as is your due,
> O Wisdom!

Repeat twice more.

Symphonia (Songs) 2

---

[35]. Kujawa-Holbrook, Sheryl A., translator. *Hildegard of Bingen: Essential Writings and Chants of a Christian Mystic—Annotated & Explained.* 1st edition, SkyLight Paths, 2016, 47.

Chapter 5
Medieval Mental Health, Ailments, and Cures

On my third morning in Germany, I came downstairs from my light and comfortable room into the kitchen/dining room of my bed and breakfast, Haus Römer Pension, where I was met by the proprietress, Elke. With it being the very beginning of tourist season, I was the only person there, so I took a seat by the window and Elke talked me through the breakfast offerings.

Elke and I had discovered that, with her limited English and my non-existent German, having a conversation via phone translation apps was the ticket. She told me I could help myself and she would bring me tea.

It was supposed to rain, and I did not have any particular plans except to explore the Abbey church and gift shop and walk down to Rüdesheim to poke around the shops. I was glad to be in the calm before the storm. I had left my own storm of pain and anxiety half a world away because I needed to be in a place where no demands were placed on me except to be. Here, in Hildegard's land, amidst the healing balm of nature and kindness of strangers, I hoped to be able to discern God's voice in the wilderness. I was no longer in shock from losing my congregation so suddenly and in such an unkind fashion, but I was unmoored and trying to navigate

Danae Ashley, M.Div., M.A., LMFT

in the fog. Yes, I had my part-time therapy practice which I loved and would continue, but who was I now without a connection to a parish? I never doubted my call to the priesthood or that I was still a priest. I did have clear discernment that I was not to return to parish ministry in this season, but did not know what else I would be doing. I just needed to hear from God what I was supposed to do with that part of my life. In that moment I was just so  sad. Clinically, I knew I was in the midst of situational depression, but I was also hurting spiritually.

Elke interrupted my thoughts by placing my tea before me and telling me through the translation app that she had something special I should take with me that day: *Nussecken*. She explained that they are usually made with hazelnuts, but she preferred walnuts. I had no idea what she was talking about until she brought some over to me. It is a German pastry called 'nut corners' made with a shortbread-like base, apricot jam, and in this case, a caramelized walnut topping, with the corners dipped in chocolate. Some of my favorite things in one pastry? I asked her to give me the recipe before I left.

After she gave me some *Nussecken* to try (perfection!), Elke asked me what I planned for my day, gave me some delightful suggestions, and then hurried over to the counter to give me a paper lunch bag. She pointed to the dazzling array of food and told me to take things for lunch and then mimed marching saying that I would be walking a lot, and I would get very hungry. She wanted me to enjoy myself and not get 'hangry.'

Elke's acting made us both laugh, but I was also moved to tears. This person, who was a stranger to me, cared about if I got hungry and if I had a good time. My friends and family cared about me, of course, but because of the situation back home, it felt more complicated for me as a person used to caring for others. But here was this woman who had no connection with me offering hospitality and making sure I was cared for in the vulnerability that she did not know I had. No wonder Elke is one of my favorite memories of this pilgrimage. Dr. Diet, Dr. Quiet, and Dr. Merryman are all important for healing, but we can never underestimate the ministry of presence. Elke set the tone for my time with Hildegard as I untangled myself on the pilgrim's path. I will forever be grateful.

Mental Health Ailments

We have examined Hildegard's holistic healing for mental health beginning with the core connection between oneself and God; family and environmental context; the Virtues and Vices; and the four personality temperaments. Moving from those broader aspects, we will now look at more specific issues that people were dealing with during Hildegard's time. Whether you are a therapist reading this, a spiritual seeker, or a person who is interested in their own mental health journey, Hildegard is rich with knowledge to lead us to deeper reflection.

Many mental health ailments are discussed between her works *Physica* and *Causae et Curae*. I am only going to focus on three in this chapter, but it is interesting to see how many observations Hildegard makes specifically about mental health. To give you an idea, here is a select list of mental health ailments in *Causae et Curae*.[1]

- Continence (sexual lust)
- Intemperance (lack of moderation/restraint)
- Phlegmatics (apathetic, sluggish)
- Fools

---

1. Hildegard of Bingen. Trans. Throop, Priscilla. *Causes and Cures of Hildegard of Bingen*. Second edition, MedievalMS, 2012.

Danae Ashley, M.Div., M.A., LMFT

- Dementia
- Desperation
- Timid People
- Suicides
- The Wrathful
- Syncope (alcoholic)
- Instability
- The Obsessed
- Sternness
- Delirium
- Excess Sleep
- Lethargy
- Sadness
- Delusion
- Forgetfulness

While mental health can be affected by physical health and vice versa, Hildegard makes specific reference to the brain and how it is affected by the humors. We have already established how the body affects one's personality development. The brain is the next obvious choice for observation. It seems that Hildegard had a basic understanding of neurological brain health and, of course, the deep connection between the heart (emotions), the mind, and the body.

The Brain[2]

The brain is affected by a person's good and bad humors, therefore it is always soft and damp. If by chance it completely dries out, it soon is brought to infirmity. Naturally very damp and fatty, it is the material of a person's awareness, wisdom, and understanding. It contains these properties, sending them forth, and drawing them back; it also holds the powers of thinking. When thoughts sit in the

---

2. Hildegard of Bingen. Trans. Throop, Priscilla. *Causes and Cures of Hildegard of Bingen*. 2nd ed., MedievalMS, 2012, 75-76.

heart, they have either sweetness or bitterness; sweetness enriches the brain and bitterness empties it. The brain has pathways, just as a chimney has openings, where the smoke is let out. Those pathways are in the eyes, ears, mouth, nostrils, where thoughts are shown. When there is sweetness in thought, the eyes, ears, and speech of a person, show happiness. When there is bitterness in thought, the eyes show tears, and speech and hearing reveal anger and sadness. A person's eyes are made in the likeness of the firmament.

Although not scientific to our modern standards, Hildegard's metaphor of the brain having chimneys to let out emotions like smoke is an astute observation and a holistic one. Neuroscience explains how our various systems are triggered by the physical and emotional information we receive.[3] Even someone who doesn't think they have a 'tell' has a tell.[4] [5] [6] Our emotions, or lack of them, shine brightly through our eyes, our speech, and what we think we hear, if one observes our responses clearly. Hildegard understood this, even if she did not have modern science to express it.

There could be a whole book on just the mental ailments and the cures that Hildegard used, but for our purposes I chose three that I see clients dealing with on a daily basis: Melancholy (Depression), Anger, and Madness (Brain Diseases). Please note that this brief exploration is for informational purposes only and

---

3. Schmid, Regina Franziska, et al. "Individual Differences in Parasympathetic Nervous System Reactivity in Response to Everyday Stress Are Associated with Momentary Emotional Exhaustion." *Scientific Reports*, vol. 14, no. 1, Nov. 2024, 26662. *www.nature.com*, https://doi.org/10.1038/s41598-024-74873-9.
4. De Ruddere, Lies, et al. "Health Care Professionals' Reactions to Patient Pain: Impact of Knowledge About Medical Evidence and Psychosocial Influences." *The Journal of Pain*, vol. 15, no. 3, Mar. 2014, 262–70. *DOI.org (Crossref)*, https://doi.org/10.1016/j.jpain.2013.11.002.
5. Verschuere, Bruno, et al. "The Ease of Lying." *Consciousness and Cognition*, vol. 20, no. 3, Sept. 2011, 908–11. *ScienceDirect*, https://doi.org/10.1016/j.concog.2010.10.023.
6. Wu, Dingcheng, et al. "Neural Correlates of Evaluations of Lying and Truth-Telling in Different Social Contexts." *Brain Research*, vol. 1389, May 2011, 115–24. *ScienceDirect*, https://doi.org/10.1016/j.brainres.2011.02.084.

does not take the place of going to your own doctor, psychiatrist, therapist, or other health care provider.

Melancholy

Many people come to psychotherapy seeking help to feel "better." They do not want to feel what they are feeling and hope that exploring their psyches will assist them in resolving whatever they are sensing in themselves. Depression is a common condition that I see in my practice and one that Hildegard did, too. She called it 'melancholy' which is an apt term for how it feels in a person's body and spirit. Here are a few symptoms of Major Depressive Disorder from the DSM-V-TR[7] that we also see reflected in Hildegard's observations:

- Depressed mood most of the day, nearly every day, as indicated by either subjective report (e.g. feels sad, empty, hopeless) or observations made by others (e.g. appears tearful).
- Markedly diminished interest or pleasure in all, or almost all, activities most of the day, nearly every day.
- Fatigue or loss of energy nearly every day.
- Psychomotor agitation or retardation nearly every day.

The following are some of the entries that Hildegard wrote describing melancholy and what she believed was going on in the body. The following entries are from *Causae et Curae*, p. 32:[8]

Melancholy is black, bitter, and gives off every ill. It sometimes creates infirmity in the head and heart, as if the veins are bursting. It brings about sadness, with doubt of all solace. A person is able to

---

7. American Psychiatric Association. *Diagnostic and Statistical Manual of Mental Disorders, Text Revision Dsm-5-Tr*. 5th edition, Amer Psychiatric Pub Inc, 2022.
8. Hildegard of Bingen. Trans. Throop, Priscilla. *Causes and Cures of Hildegard of Bingen*. Second edition, MedievalMS, 2012.

have no joy, which belongs to heavenly life and to the consolation of the present life. This melancholy is natural to everyone from the original suggestion of the devil, when the human transgressed God's order in eating the apple. From this food, melancholy grew in Adam and all his kind, and it stirred up disease in humans.

There are other people who are sad, timid, and vague in their minds, so in them is not right constitution or state. They are like a strong wind, which is harmful to all plants and fruits. Whence phlegm grows in them, which is neither damp nor thick, but lukewarm. It is like livor and is tenacious, stretching out in length, like gum resin. It brings about melancholy, which arose from the serpent's breath in the first birth from the seed of Adam, since Adam followed the serpent's advice about food.

The first few sentences in the first passage are a good summation of how depression can be experienced. It feels like it could be from the Devil—an outside force that is relentless in keeping a person swathed in a cocoon of hopelessness. Clients describe it as a dark cloud, saying that trying to even do a simple act, like getting out of bed, feels like you are moving through molasses in a fog. Even the body aches. It also feels like it will never end. Typical of Hildegard's understanding of the genesis of all disease, she relates this to the Fall of Adam and Eve in both passages.

a pilgrim ponders

Have I ever felt the symptoms Hildegard describes? What helped me feel better?

Often melancholy rises up in a person and diffuses a smoking vapor in him. This contracts his veins, blood, and flesh until it stops spreading through the body, that is, until it ceases. But it happens very often, that bile is overabundant in a person and, in its superfluity, spreads through the person's body. And so the

> *person suffers as if pungent fissures in his flesh, until the excess bile abates.*[9]
>
> *When bile has greater power than melancholy, a person easily tames his anger; when melancholy has greater power than bile, the person is prone to anger, easily flying into a rage. Just as vinegar made from good wine becomes strong and sour, so bile increases from good, sweet foods and decreases from bad ones. Melancholy decreases from good, sweet foods, and increases from foods which are bad, bitter, unclean, and badly prepared, as well as from humors of various maladies.*[10]

Hildegard's connection between melancholy and anger is insightful. Excessive anger or irritation can be a sign of depression. I see this in my practice, especially in those who do not feel emotionally safe expressing sadness or depressive feelings,[11] are unable to identify depressive sensations within themselves, and/or see sadness/depressive feelings as a "weakness." We know now that depression can be caused by chemical imbalances in the brain that are either organic to the person and/or arise from events that happen, such as job loss, loss of health, and other life events, and can be short-term or pervasive.

Healing Melancholy

Today we treat depression mainly with therapy and medication —including ketamine and psilocybin treatments with trained practitioners. Hildegard used common medieval treatments, some of which contradicted each other, others of which might have killed someone (eliminating the problem altogether), and a few that may

---

9. Hildegard of Bingen. Trans. Throop, Priscilla. *Causes and Cures of Hildegard of Bingen.* 2nd ed., MedievalMS, 2012, 118.
10. Ibid., 119.
11. "Behaviors in Men That Could Be Signs of Depression." *Mayo Clinic,* https://www.mayoclinic.org/diseases-conditions/depression/in-depth/male-depression/art-20046216. Accessed 19 Mar. 2025.

have eased the symptoms. Here are some of her remedies from Hildegard's *Physica*.[12] Please do not try any of them at home:

> *And a person in whom melancholy rages, who has a fierce mind, and who is always sad, should also frequently drink wine cooked with the arum root. His melancholy and fever will diminish.*[13]
>
> *Rue* (rutha) *grows more from the strong, full liveliness of the earth than from heat...A person who is melancholic will be better when he eats rue after a meal.*[14]
>
> *A person whom melancholy is harming should pound fennel to a liquid and rub it often on his forehead, temples, chest, and stomach. His melancholy will stop.*[15]
>
> *Anyone oppressed by melancholy with a discontented mind, which then harms his lungs, should cook violets in pure wine. He should strain this through a cloth, add a bit of galingale, and as much licorice as he wants, and so make spiced wine. When he drinks it, it will check the melancholy, make him happy, and heal his lungs.*[16]
>
> *Primrose* (hymelsloszel) *is hot. All its vital energy is from the sharpness of the sun. Now, certain plants are strengthened by the sun, others by the moon, and certain others from the sun and moon together. But this plant takes its strength especially from the power of the sun, whence it checks melancholy. When melancholy rises in a person, it makes him sad and agitated in his moods. It makes him pour forth words against God. Airy spirits notice this, and rush to him, and by their persuasion turn him toward insanity. This person should place primrose on his flesh, near his heart, until it*

---

12. Hildegard of Bingen. *Hildegard von Bingen's Physica: The Complete English Translation of Her Classic Work on Health and Healing.* Translated by Priscilla Throop, First Edition, Healing Arts Press, 1998.
13. Ibid., 31.
14. Ibid., 37.
15. Ibid., 40.
16. Ibid., 54.

> *warms him up. The airy spirits dread the primrose's sun-given power and will cease their torment.*[17]
>
> *The Elm tree: If someone burns this wood alone, heats water with it, and takes a bath in this water, it will take away malignity and bad will, give him benevolence, and make his mind happy. That tree has a certain prosperity in its nature, so that spirits of the air are unable to move their phantasms, wrongs, and illusions through it with their many wrathful confrontations.*[18]
>
> *One who is melancholic, so that he has a heaviness and listlessness of the mind, should frequently eat ostrich liver. It will diminish his melancholy and, by lightening his mind, make it pleasant and charming.*[19]

It is unclear where Hildegard would have gotten an ostrich, but this is an illustration of the far-reaching connection between Benedictine monasteries and their study of medicine. You will see the occasional element in Hildegard's cures that does not fit with the German landscape or the Rhine Valley specifically. Unsurprisingly, many of her medicines include plants and wine—two things in abundance where she lived.

Adlerian Link

Adler wrote about melancholy as "Melancholia as Aggression" which is an interesting observation about how this internal process can be turned outward. He defines it this way:

> *Melancholia develops in individuals whose method of living has from early childhood been dependent upon the achievements and the support of others. Such individuals will always try to lean on others and will not scorn the use of exaggerated hints at their own*

---

17. Ibid., 91.
18. Ibid., 130.
19. Ibid., 178.

inadequacy to force the support, adjustment, and submissiveness of others...By concretizing their subjective inferiority feeling, melancholiacs openly or implicitly raise the claim to higher "disability compensation."[20]

Adler's viewpoint is to always look at how behavior is useful to the person's lifestyle. Unconsciously, we develop ways when we are young to survive our family of origin and get through life—some are functional, and others become maladaptive and dysfunctional over time. "Melancholia thus presents itself as an attempt and device to achieve the goal of superiority by detours. As in any neurosis and psychosis this is done through voluntary payment of the 'cost of war.'"[21]

For Adler, treating melancholia means activating social interest. This would include asking for an Early Recollection (ER) to understand where the melancholia began, finding strengths and building on them (from the ER or other conversation), and giving a small, doable social interest assignment such as making a friend a cup of tea. The therapist themselves continues to hold the patient with unconditional positive regard and offers encouragement along the way. Note: Treating chronic, severe depression caused by chemical imbalances in the brain requires additional methods such as medication or other drug-related treatments and therapy; the same goes for treating depression caused by insomnia, although a different type of therapy—Cognitive Behavioral Therapy for Insomnia (CBT-I)—can help.

---

20. Ansbacher, Heinz L., and Rowena R. Ansbacher, eds. *The Individual Psychology of Alfred Adler: A Systematic Presentation in Selections from His Writings.* Harper Perennial, 1964, 319.
21. Ibid., 321.

Danae Ashley, M.Div., M.A., LMFT

Anger

> *"Anger is the worst fault and is, as it were, the heart of the devil. Sometimes anger hides itself in the grotto of a dove and then attacks a man in his own familiar territory where it destroys the protection of his understanding...Anger is similar to a stubborn thief. It gnashes its teeth at people because of their worthy gifts from God...Anger is like a dragon that burns everything wherever it goes..."*[22]

Irritation, rage, fury, outrage, annoyance—all of these forms of anger are part of the human experience. Hildegard saw anger as a mental ailment that also affected the soul. Her descriptions of anger in *Liber Vitae Meritorum* above describe what I see in my psychotherapy practice—anger is destructive in people's lives. Notice the details about the state of the soul and of the body when someone is angry from the following observations of Hildegard in *Causae et Curae*:[23]

> *Some people are naturally prone to anger. When their soul, affected by weariness, is in quiet repose, sometimes, from their anger, a deficiency befalls them, whence their body is oppressed. The soul recovers its powers and resurges. In other people, it often happens that their souls, affected by weariness, are in quiet repose, and their bodies are oppressed by some distress. These souls also, having been stirred up, recover their former powers and return. Bodies of other people are constrained by impatience or doubt when their souls are silent, having been oppressed by*

---

22. Hildegard of Bingen and Bruce W. Hozeski. *The Book of the Rewards of Life: Liber Vitae Meritorum.* Oxford University Press, 1997, 59.
23. Hildegard of Bingen. Trans. Throop, Priscilla. *Causes and Cures of Hildegard of Bingen.* 2nd ed., MedievalMS, 2012.

labor and weariness. Their drowsing souls, stirred up, rise back to their original powers.[24]

The blood of a person, whose face gets red when he is angry, boils from bile which is led to his face. He is suddenly moved to great anger, but it is quickly suppressed, as any great fervor which quickly subsides. This anger does not harm him much, nor does his body get dry. And often, not avenging himself, it passes through without vindication. But a person who grows pale in the face when he is moved to anger, has ire of such a kind that the melancholy, stirred up in him, does not move his blood, but gradually disturbs his humors. The person becomes cold, and his powers are impaired and grow soft. He grows pale in his face, covering his anger. Meanwhile the ill will of bitter vengeance rises in him, which endures because he is not able to restrain himself, but rather vindicates his anger.[25]

Other people are so constituted that they very often grow hot in anger. The anger in these people often moves all their blood in a great, bloody inundation. From this, a vapor-like humor touches their brain and makes them insane, so that even their knowledge diminishes. Sometimes, when these people are moved to anger and aggravated by worldly troubles, the devil notices and terrifies them by his breath of suggestion. Whence the soul sinks down fatigued and withdraws. The body, failing, falls and lies in its deficiency until the soul again arises, its strengths recovered. People vexed by this evil, seem angry in appearance as well as in movement. Falling to the ground, they sometimes emit an unnatural sound. This disease [epilepsy] manifests very rarely and is suppressed with difficulty.[26]

---

24. Ibid., 126.
25. Ibid., 119.
26. Ibid., 126-127.

Danae Ashley, M.Div., M.A., LMFT

Once again, I find Hildegard's connection between anger and sadness insightful. In modern psychotherapy, we understand that anger is an emotional response to something tender underneath being hurt. Sometimes it is a fear, as in a fear that someone will stop loving you. Sometimes it is a loss, as in the loss of an important relationship or a dream. Sadness can manifest as anger when a person does not feel comfortable being sad and anger is easier to access as an emotion. From *Causae et Curae*:

> *When a person's soul senses something adverse to itself and to its body, it contracts the heart, liver and veins. Something like mist rises up around the heart, clouding it, and the person becomes sad. After sadness, anger rises up. When the person sees, hears, or recognizes something which has caused sadness, the mist of sadness, which occupied his heart, creates a warm vapor in all his humors and around his gall bladder. It stirs up the bile. Thus anger silently rises from the bitterness of bile. When the person does not end his anger, but silently bears it, he holds back the bile. If anger will not have ceased, the vapor, stretching itself to melancholy, stirs it up, and it sends out a very black mist. This, passing to the bile, twists from it a very bitter vapor. This mist, passing with the vapor to the person's brain {stirs up contrary humors, which} first make him ill in the head. Then they descend to the stomach and strike its veins and the inside of his stomach, and make the person as if delirious. And so a person, as if unknowingly, brings about anger. A person rages more from anger than from any other infirmity of dementia. A person also contracts certain serious illnesses from anger, because when contrary humors from bile and melancholy are stirred up very often in a person, they sometimes make him sick. If a person lacked the bitterness of bile and the blackness of melancholy, he would always be healthy.*[27]

---

27. Hildegard of Bingen. Trans. Throop, Priscilla. *Causes and Cures of Hildegard of Bingen*. 2nd ed., MedievalMS, 2012, 118-119.

My Sap is Rising

a pilgrim ponders

Have I ever hidden sadness or fear beneath anger? What happened when I did this?

Hildegard's grasp on how anger affects the body was impressive. She named what happens in the body when a person holds in their anger and bears a grudge. It makes everything bitter—their brain and their stomach. Anger can also make a person sick with what she called "certain serious illnesses." Anger is a serious health issue not only to Hildegard, but for our culture today. Anger hurts a person on multiple levels, including their connection with others and with God. We cannot be whole when we live in anger and Hildegard was right to include it as a disease.

Healing Anger

Hildegard brings us intriguing cures for anger, and she had different remedies for the various types. From *Causae et Curae*:

> *If anyone is moved to anger or sadness, he should readily heat wine on the fire, mix it with moderately cold water, and drink it to suppress the vapor of melancholy which has aroused the anger in him.*[28]
>
> *A person so moved by anger that he becomes sick, should dry laurel berries on a hot tile, then pulverize them. He should also pulverize sage and marjoram after they have dried in the sun, and place this, with the laurel berry powder, in a small box, so there is more laurel berry than sage, and more sage than marjoram. He should place it near his nose, on account of the pleasant odor. Mixing some of this powder with a bit of cold wine, he should anoint his forehead, temples, and chest. Laurel berries have a warm, dry dryness [possibly should be dry 'vital fluid'], and this moistens the humors which anger dries up in a person. The heat of*

---

28. Ibid., 158.

> *marjoram sedates the brain moved by anger, and the dry heat of sage gathers the humors which anger destroyed. When laurel berries are dried over a hot tile (on account of the healthfulness in it) and placed with marjoram and sage, which had been dried in the sun (on account of its strength) they, so tempered, ease this infirmity with their good heat. The powder of these things, mixed with the natural sweetness of the unheated wine, soothes the veins on the forehead, temples, and chest, which had been disturbed by anger, as described.*[29]

Hildegard recognizes the physical effects of anger and prescribes physical remedies as well as spiritual. Anger is also considered a vice, so moving toward the virtue of peace through prayer and behavior changes might also be part of the healing path.

Adlerian Link

Adler believed that emotions were "psychological movement forms, limited in time"[30] and there were two types of emotions: socially disjunctive and socially conjunctive.

> *The disjunctive emotions* (trennende Affekte), *such as anger, sorrow, or fear are not mysterious phenomena which cannot be interpreted. They appear always where they serve a purpose corresponding to the life method or guiding line of the individual. Their purpose is to bring about a change of the situation in favor of the individual.*[31]
>
> *In the socially conjunctive emotions* (verbindende Affekte), *we clearly see the social relationship. The emotion of joy, for example, cannot stand in isolation…The entire attitude is engaging. It*

---

29. Bingen, op. cit., 158.
30. Ansbacher, Heinz L., and Rowena R. Ansbacher, editors. *The Individual Psychology of Alfred Adler: A Systematic Presentation in Selections from His Writings.* Harper Perennial, 1964, 227.
31. Ibid., 227.

> *is extending the hand so to speak, a warmth which radiates toward the other person and is intended to elevate him as well. All the elements of union are present in this emotion.*[32]

For Adler, we can only heal by understanding the individual and this is not done in isolation. Emotions such as anger are symptoms of something deeper happening that we must explore, with no two persons giving the symptom the same significance. "But," Adler writes, "there is one assumption we can make in all cases: a symptom is connected with the individual's struggle to reach a chosen [final, fictional] goal."[33] Once this fictional goal is understood, a person can catch themselves doing the behavior that unconsciously moves toward this goal which gives opportunity to change course, leading to healing.

Madness

Madness or insanity is something that Hildegard discerned in a variety of ways. From her observations, she seems to have been talking about brain diseases which can come from an illness, virus, or traumatic brain injury. Here are a few examples:

> *If the damp and tepid, which then are the livor of the foamy and dry, surpass moderation, the damp is soon rolled around like a wheel, and plunges the person sometimes into water, sometimes into fire; the tepid sends him into madness. Such a person becomes mad, since his knowledge has vanished. He is neither fully healthy nor fully ill.*[34]
>
> Insanity. *When the aforementioned afflictions [headache,*

---

32. Ibid., 227.
33. Ansbacher, Heinz L., and Rowena R. Ansbacher, editors. *The Individual Psychology of Alfred Adler: A Systematic Presentation in Selections from His Writings.* Harper Perennial, 1964, 330.
34. Hildegard of Bingen. Trans. Throop, Priscilla. *Causes and Cures of Hildegard of Bingen.* 2nd ed., MedievalMS, 2012, 44-45.

> *migraine, and vertigo] occur all at once so that they rage simultaneously in a human's head, then they drive him to insanity, overpower him completely and let him lose his right understanding, just as a ship shaken by storms will burst into pieces. Therefore many people will believe that this person is possessed by a demon, which is not the case. Demons, though, rush toward this severe affliction and pain and lie in ambush, because driving someone insane is part of their function. But they have no power over this person's words, because he is not possessed by a demon. Yet if by divine permission a demon has power within a person over his words, then this demon, taking the place of the Holy Spirit, will be ravaging there until God expels him, just as God has driven him out from heaven.*[35]
>
> Insanity instigated by anger. *Other people are so constituted that they very often grow hot in anger. The anger in these people often moves all their blood in a great, bloody inundation. From this, a vapor-like humor touches their brain and makes them insane, so that even their knowledge diminishes.*[36]

In the second passage, Hildegard distinguishes the difference between insanity in the brain and possession by a demon. In modern times, we look back at the medieval era and think they thought any kind of mental illness was demon possession. Clearly, from Hildegard's observations, this is not true. A certain type of madness was caused by demon possession with discernable characteristics. Disease could be identified within the body through other explanations such as the humors or external factors such as worms or blunt force trauma.

---

35. Hildegard of Bingen. *Hildegard of Bingen: On Natural Philosophy and Medicine.* Translated by Margret Berger, D. S. Brewer, 1999, 70-71.
36. Ibid., 126.

Healing Madness

We throw around the terms 'insane' and 'crazy' in contemporary times when someone does not follow the social norms, is in the throes of psychosis, has a brain injury, or is just having a bad day. While we have modern science to help us figure out what is happen-

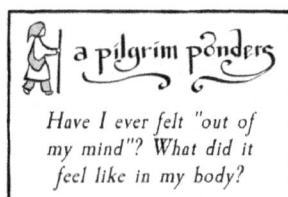

a pilgrim ponders

Have I ever felt "out of my mind"? What did it feel like in my body?

ing, there is still much that cannot be explained. Hildegard came up against the same limitations and did her best to help who was in front of her. We can see that this was a prominent issue based on how often it is mentioned in her work and the variety of remedies for it. How is this different from how we treat those whom we deem insane now with our multitude of drugs and therapies? For Hildegard, restoring an insane person to sanity and back to the community echoed Jesus' healings (and exorcisms) in the Gospel stories. Is this the goal of treatment today?

Hildegard's instructions on healing madness are some of the more colorful. You can get the sense of medieval medicine in her recipes with ingredients like wolf broth, stone broth, and wearing a lion skin. Again, a nod to the broad reach of Benedictine monasteries and the sharing of knowledge and manuscripts is clear. The following are a selection of remedies. As with all her other remedies, please do not try these at home:

> *If someone's brain has gotten cold, so that he has become mad from it, take laurel berries and reduce them to a powder. Mix the powdered berries with wheat flour and water, and knead this. Having shaved the head, place this dough over his whole head. Tie a felt cap over it, until his head warms up inside, and let him go to sleep; this conveys heat to the brain. When the dough dries out,*

prepare more in the same way and place it on his head. Do this often, and he will recover his senses.[37]

If anyone's knowledge and understanding are lost from many diverse thoughts, so that he has become a madman, he should cook costmary[38] *[Tanacetum balsamita aka balsam herb or mint geranium] and three times as much fennel in water. Having thrown out the herbs, he should frequently drink the water, cooled. The juice of the costmary constricts and restrains bad humors, so they don't become exceedingly wayward; it returns a person to his senses. The fennel juice brings forth correctly balanced happiness. These herbs, mixed together and cooked in sweet water, make the person return to his understanding...He should drink the herbal brew, described above, and beer. These keep in check his destitute humors and senses, and overthrow the fury of madness. He should cover his head with a cap made of felt or pure wool until his brain, cooled by the destitute humors, gradually and gently becomes warm. This should not be done suddenly and excessively, lest he get much worse from the sudden great heat.*[39]

One whose brain is afflicted should cook pennyroyal in wine and place it, so warmed, around his entire head. He should tie a cloth over it. This will warm his brain and suppress his madness.[40]

White dock[41] *(sichterwurtz alba) [Veratrum album L.] has the same nature as the black dock except that the black is harsher*

---

37. Hildegard of Bingen. Trans. Throop, Priscilla. *Causes and Cures of Hildegard of Bingen*. 2nd ed., MedievalMS, 2012, 134.
38. Costmary was used as a diuretic, laxative, and antipyretic (fever reducer). The herb was used in making potpourri and was tied in bundles with lavender to add fragrance to bedding.
39. Bingen, op. cit., 136.
40. Hildegard of Bingen. *Hildegard von Bingen's Physica: The Complete English Translation of Her Classic Work on Health and Healing*. Translated by Priscilla Throop, 1st ed., Healing Arts Press, 1998, 66.
41. People take white hellebore for cholera, gout, and high blood pressure. White hellebore is sometimes applied directly to the affected area for herpes outbreaks. In manufacturing, white hellebore is used as an insecticide against flies and mosquitoes. https://www.rxlist.com/supplements/white_hellebore.htm#:~:text=People%20take%20white%20hellebore%20for,insecticide%20against%20flies%20and%20mosquitoes.

than the white. White dock, mixed with wild thyme and fennel and lard...chases madness from a person. It is a valuable addition to other medicinal mixtures and ointments.[42]

Draw off the skin of the lion, from the neck, over the head and its crown. Save it. If someone is mad from any infirmity in his head, he should warm up from having that fleece over his head, and he will recover his senses.[43]

If someone, because of weakness of diseases, should be mad in the head and insane, shave the hair from his head and cook a wolf in water, having thrown away its head and intestines. Wash the head of the mad one in a broth of this water, with his eyes, ears, and mouth tied with a cloth, lest any of it enter these places. If any of the broth enters his body, he would go more crazy, since it would be as a poison to him. Do this for three days, although the madness is great, he will recover his senses. If he does not allow you to bind his eyes, ears, and nose with a cloth, then dip a linen cloth in the broth, and dampen his head with the warm cloth. Allow it to lie on his head for a little while. After doing this for three days, he will return to his senses. When he is better, wash his head in warm wine, so the richness will be washed and removed from his head.[44]

If someone is insane, use this unguent to anoint his temples and neck, so that it touches neither the top of his head nor the brain, which might be harmed by its strength. This restores his right mind and good health.[45]

You will notice there are several solutions of shaving and/or then putting something on or around a person's head. Presumably shaving their head would allow the treatment—wool, lion's skin, wolf broth, or unguent—to be closer to the site of where the mental issue originates: the brain. This could be helpful for a person to feel more comfortable but does not heal what is happening in the brain.

---

42. Bingen, op. cit., 68.
43. Bingen, op. cit., 207.
44. Bingen, op. cit., 217.
45. Bingen, op. cit., 82.

Danae Ashley, M.Div., M.A., LMFT

Plus, I am certain that wolf's broth and the skin of a lion are difficult, if not illegal to acquire in today's time, in addition to not healing a brain disease. Let us see what else Hildegard suggests from *Physica*:

> *A person who has epilepsy or is a lunatic will be better if he always has an agate next to his skin. People are often born with these infirmities; they even attract them from a superfluity of bad humors and pestilence...Also, a lunatic, when he knows his illness is impending, should, three days before, place this stone in water. On the fourth day, he should take it out and gently heat the water. He should cook in it all the foods which he will eat while he is in his senseless state. If he does this for five months, he will recover his sense and good health, unless God forbids it. He will be resuscitated by the virtue of this stone in gently heated water. Lest he be injured by the heat of this stone, his foods should be prepared with this water and his drinks prepared in the way described. By their moderation, and by the power of God, the humors which brought insanity to him will be sedated.*[46]

Hildegard used an agate heated in water for this recipe because she believed that gemstones generally were created with heat and water in the earth, containing energy and moisture that will help balance the humors. Gemstones also had a spiritual element in frightening off the Devil.[47] Notice her statement "unless God forbids it." This is common in Hildegard's recipes because the basis of all her healing comes from God first. This also protects the healer from trouble because if their remedy does not work, they can attribute it to God's will and not the ineffectiveness of their treatment.

---

46. Hildegard of Bingen. *Hildegard von Bingen's Physica: The Complete English Translation of Her ClassicWork on Health and Healing.* Translated by Priscilla Throop, 1st ed., Healing Arts Press, 1998, 150-151.
47. *St. Hildegard on Gemstones – Unam Sanctam Catholicam.* https://unamsanctam catholicam.com/2022/04/25/st-hildegard-on-gemstones/. Accessed 20 Mar. 2025.

Adlerian Link

As we have established, Adler believed that each person is a unique individual and has a creative way of going about reaching their final, fictional goal. "We look upon symptoms as creations, as works of art,"[48] Adler states. If a person is behaving insanely, Adler would look at not only the behaviors, but also the physical state to rule out physical trauma to the brain or a disease such as dementia. If a physical ailment is not present, then Adler would turn to examining the style of life and how the behaviors are fulfilling the goal.

For example, in cases of schizophrenia and other psychoses, Adler held that they have the goal of Godlikeness. The person was not only striving to be the center of attention, but already believes they are. "This goal of personal superiority blocks the approach to reality. The end result, and logical culmination of such a life-line is, of course, total isolation in an asylum."[49]

Adler admits that it is a "very difficult art"[50] to cure these cases but holds optimism that if social interest can be mustered, the patient can be won and healed with "patience and the kindliest and friendliest manner."[51] While there are no cures for schizophrenia and other psychoses, we currently manage them with personalized combinations of antipsychotic medication and psychosocial interventions, including group therapy (Adler would approve of the social interest).

Magic and the Devil's Hatred

Beginning with Biblical accounts and throughout Christian history, including today, people have been impacted spiritually by what

---

48. Ansbacher, Heinz L., and Rowena R. Ansbacher, editors. *The Individual Psychology of Alfred Adler: A Systematic Presentation in Selections from His Writings.* Harper Perennial, 1964, 330.
49. Ibid., 314.
50. Ibid., 316.
51. Ibid., 316.

they believed were evil spirits not related to mental illness. In the Gospels, Jesus performed exorcisms and taught his disciples to do the same.[52]

In Hildegard's time, magic and the Devil were real to many people and they feared both. It is no surprise that she had remedies for insanity through magic and protections from magic and the Devil's hatred. There is one characteristic that is specifically mentioned which would prove that the ailment was from outside evil and not an organic brain disease: being "tortured by phantasms." She did not describe what 'magic' or 'evil words' would be done or said explicitly, but I imagine that if physical observation of symptoms did not bring conclusive reasons for insanity, magic or evil words would be the logical explanation in the medieval world.

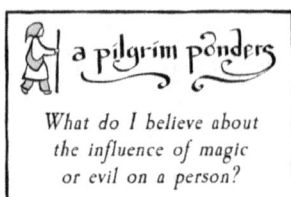

a pilgrim ponders

What do I believe about the influence of magic or evil on a person?

> Insanity through magic: *If someone through magic or by evil words is rendered insane, take the earth which is around the roots of this tree [Plum Tree] and warm it vigorously in the fire, until it burns a little bit. When it has burned a bit in the fire, place rue and a little less pennyroyal on it. Let it absorb their sap and odor. If you do not have pennyroyal, place fresh fenugreek on it. If it is winter, place on it the seeds of these herbs, moderately warmed. After the person has eaten, place this, with the herbs, on his head, naked stomach, and naked sides, and tie it with a cloth. Put him in bed and cover him with clothing, so that he might sweat a bit with that*

---

52. For exorcisms in the New Testament see the Gospels and the Acts of the Apostles: the demoniac in the synagogue (Luke 4:33-37), the Gerasene demoniac (Mark 5:1-20, Matthew 8:26-39), the Syro-Phoenician woman's daughter (Mark 7:24-30, Matt 15:21-28), the possessed boy (Mark 9: 14-29, Matthew 17:14-21; Luke 9:37-42), the man made mute by demon (Luke 11:14, Matthew 9:32) and a woman possessed with a crippling spirit (Luke 13:10-17), exorcism of the slave girl (Acts 16:16-18), and an unsuccessful one, the sons of Sceva (Acts 19:13-20).

earth. *Do this for three or five days, and he will be better. For when the ancient serpent hears magic and evil words, he takes them up and sets traps for the one for whom they were said, unless God stops him.*[53]

The Devil's Hatred. *Since the devil hates a person's virtue, he also hates all virtuous creatures, animals, or plants, which are clean and useful. A person vexed by a diabolical phantasm, day and night, whether awake or sleeping, should seek a God-given remedy.*[54]

Healing from Magic and the Devil's Hatred

It makes sense that Hildegard would use a prayer ritual as part of the remedy for healing from evil spirits and visions. This is a spiritual ailment that is affecting the body, so there would need to be both spiritual and physical treatments. Here is one treatment with a ritual from *Physica*:

If a person is mad or in any way tortured by phantasms, smear the Magnesian stone with his saliva, then rub the top of his head and his forehead with the stone, and say, 'You, raging evil, cede to that virtue by which God changed the strength of the devil who fell from heaven to human goodness.' He will recover his senses.[55]

The next two herbal remedies are also from *Physica*. They made me pause to think about what churches and psychotherapists might want to plant around their spaces for protection!

---

53. Hildegard of Bingen. *Hildegard von Bingen's Physica: The Complete English Translation of Her Classic Work on Health and Healing*. Translated by Priscilla Throop, 1st ed., Healing Arts Press, 1998, 112.
54. Hildegard of Bingen. Trans. Throop, Priscilla. *Causes and Cures of Hildegard of Bingen*. 2nd ed., MedievalMS, 2012, 117.
55. Hildegard of Bingen. *Hildegard von Bingen's Physica: The Complete English Translation of Her Classic Work on Health and Healing*. Translated by Priscilla Throop, 1st ed., Healing Arts Press, 1998, 152.

> *Fern (farn) is very hot and dry and has a little bit of juice in it. It holds within itself great power, namely such a power that the devil flees from it.*[56]
>
> *Lavender (lavendula) is hot and dry, having very little moisture. It is not effective for a person to eat, but it does have a strong odor. If a person with many lice frequently smells lavender, the lice will die. Its odor clears the eyes [since it possesses the power of the strongest aromas and the usefulness of the most bitter ones. It curbs very many evil things and, because of it, malign spirits are terrified].*[57]

There is much that the scope of this work did not explore regarding physical health and their cures. Hildegard has many followers of her diet and health protocols that you can find elsewhere. For our purposes, I highlight the unique and holistic approaches she had to diagnosing and healing common mental health issues that continue to plague us today. It is worth noting that there is a difference between healing and curing. Healing occurs holistically but does not necessarily mean that a person is cured. For example, a person came to Hildegard with the symptoms of cancer, and she treated them for the pain and alleviated suffering, while also praying for them and encouraging them to follow a virtuous path to God. In doing these things, the person had peace and felt healed but was not cured.

Conversely, a person could be cured of an infected wound but is not healed because they go back to a life of vice and aggression. Curing is a medical resolution, but healing requires a spiritual resolution. Hildegard's psychotherapeutic approach always begins and ends with God.

---

56. Ibid., 29.
57. Ibid., 25.

Pilgrim's Reflection

1. What resonated with you in Hildegard's descriptions of Melancholy, Anger, and Madness? Do you prefer her descriptions or modern-day diagnoses?

2. Adler believed that social interest is primary to mental health. He gave the image of a vertical line of superiority in which one climbs the ladder of life, not caring who they step on along the way; and a horizontal line of social interest, where we hold hands with those on either side and help each other along the way.

Reflect on when you have been on the vertical line and who you may have hurt along the way. Have you been able to make amends? Then reflect on when you have been part of the horizontal line. Whose hands were you holding? Who was helping you on your journey of life?

3. As we learned from Adler, our initial disjunctive emotion, such as anger, points to something deeper underneath. In this exercise, you can explore what might be behind your anger or fear.

- Gather together a piece of paper and colors or get some air-dry clay if you prefer a more tactile experience.
- Using your non-dominant hand, draw a large box on the page that represents a big emotion you are experiencing that you would like to unpack. (For clay: Construct a hollow box.)
- Write or make marks inside the box of all the different things that are beneath the surface of this big emotion. (For clay: Create small balls or other constructs to represent those things and put them inside the box.) Ask questions and stay gently curious.
    - Example: If the big emotion is anger, you may ask, "What is this really about? What do I fear? What are the things that fill me with sadness? What is the anger alerting me to—a boundary crossed? A need not being met?
- Draw a lid on the box (For clay: Make a lid.) Now you can decide which thing to take out of the box to reflect on one at a time.
- As you take one thing out at a time to reflect on, you may wish to create a new symbol to represent the time and care you have taken in paying attention to that aspect of the underlying big emotion.

4. What in your life has been healed but not cured?

5. Hildegard used recipes for healing, including one called "Cookies of Joy" or "Nerve Cookies" to "help calm all bitterness of the heart and mind, open your heart and impaired senses, and

make your mind cheerful" (*Physica*, Book 1, Chapter 21). The recipe includes flour (many use spelt given how highly Hildegard valued its properties – "spelt is the best grain"), cinnamon, nutmeg, and cloves. I was delighted to find these at the Eibingen Abbey gift shop where the nuns continue her tradition. Dr. Victoria Sweet has a recipe for these on her website called "St. Hildegard's Anti-Depressant Cookies," *Tasting History with Max Miller* on YouTube also has one, and you can find it in a variety of places on the internet. I encourage you to try them!

Danae Ashley, M.Div., M.A., LMFT

Benediction

Our healing means we are becoming. Hildegard's antiphon to the Holy Spirit speaks to this:

> The Spirit of God
> is a life that bestows life,
> root of the world tree
> and wind in its boughs.
>
> Scrubbing out sins
> she rubs oil into wounds.
>
> She is glistening life
> alluring all praise,
> all awakening,
> all resurrecting.

Symphonia 141[58]

---

58. Craine, Renate. *Hildegard: Prophet of the Cosmic Christ*. Crossroad, 1997, 63.

My Sap is Rising

Group/embodied option: Split your group in half with one half embodying the first stanza and the other half the second. All join in the third stanza.

> The Spirit of God (*Swirl hands above head*)
> is a life that bestows life, (*Bring hands down, laying them gently as if on someone's head in blessing*)
> root of the world tree (*Release hands and stomp twice, feeling rooted and solid*)
> and wind in its boughs. (*Wave arms like a tree in the wind*)
>
> Scrubbing out sins, (*Make scrubbing motions on body*)
> she rubs oil into wounds. (*Make gentle rubbing motions on body*)
>
> She is glistening life (*Flick all fingers out like rinsing water off them or flashing like a light*)
> alluring all praise, (*Bring fingertips to mouth and motion like you are blowing a kiss*)
> all-awakening, (*Stretch your limbs, roll your head like you getting up after a long nap*)
> all-resurrecting. (*End in star position—feet spread, arms up at a diagonal, head lifted to the sky*)

Danae Ashley, M.Div., M.A., LMFT

The Spirit of God   is a life that bestows life,

root of the world tree   and wind in its boughs.

Scrubbing out sins,   she rubs oil into wounds.

She is glistening life,   alluring   all praise,

all-awakening   all-resurrecting.

Chapter 6
Rituals for Healing

The buzzing sound grew louder as I walked further on the cloister path toward the entry to the Eibingen Abbey church. As I got closer, I could see the mosaic of the Cross of St. Benedict on the entry above and heavy bronze doors inlaid with the same Cross in a repeated pattern on their panels. To my right, the life-size bronze sculpture of Hildegard by sculptor Karlheinz Oswald gazed out over the garden with a feather at her feet. The garden bordering the path was alive with bees feasting on the spring blooming herbs and flowers. This happy sound felt like the bees were adding their prayers to the prayers I was about to make at the Vespers (5:00 pm) service that Elke encouraged me to attend.

But when I got to the doors, they were locked. A notice printed on red paper announced a change to the schedule. It read (with the help of my translation app):

Danae Ashley, M.Div., M.A., LMFT

> The festive service with image meditation and candlelight procession will take place on Wednesday, May 10, 2023 at 6:00 pm in the parish church of St. Hildegard in Eibingen. Afterwards, everyone is invited to a get together in the parish hall...We cordially invite all visitors to join us at the festive service in the Eibingen parish church!

I figured out pretty quickly that the church they were inviting me to was the one that I stopped in at on my way up the steep switchbacks to the Abbey. The one that held Hildegard's relics. There must be some special feast day I was not aware of, so taking another glance at the Hildegard statue with its feather at her feet, I reminded myself I was a "feather on the breath of God" and started walking down to the church.

This time when I entered the parish church, there were many people there. I sat in the back because the service was in German and I wanted to take my cues from others for what to do. The nuns from the Abbey were there, which I found out later was a rare occasion, as they are cloistered. When I translated the bulletin, I discovered that this was a celebration of the anniversary of Hildegard finally becoming canonized as a saint on May 10, 2012. I had no idea that I had arrived on such an important date. I knew her feast day was September 17 but had not thought further than that.

The room was full of joy and excitement. A government official of the town spoke, as well as a sister of the Abbey. They both spoke passionately and with a tone of celebration. Everyone was smiling. We were then invited to come out of our pews, down the center aisle with a processional hymn in hand and take a candle that someone lit for you on your way out the side door. We processed into the spring evening going around the church and coming back into the sanctuary all the way up to the altar singing:

Ave, Sankt Hildegardis, du heilige, hehre Frau!
Aus hohen Himmelshallen auf uns hernieder schau!
Erfleh uns Gottes Gnad, dass unbeirrt
wir wallen des Heiles rechten Pfad. (Verse 1)

Translation:
Hail, Saint Hildegard, holy noble lady!
Look down upon us from the high halls of heaven!
Beg for God's grace that we
may walk steadfastly on the right path of salvation.

We stood around Hildegard's reliquary with our candles, singing. When the hymn finished, everyone put their candles around the base of the dais the reliquary was on, and someone did a final prayer. Afterward, they gave out prayer cards and icon prints of St. Hildegard with St. Benedict for a donation and I took one that I rolled up and stuck in the inside of my backpack for the remainder of my pilgrimage. I got it framed as soon as I returned.

My first encounter with Hildegard's relics was when I was alone. Being with a group of people venerating her so jubilantly was powerful in a different way. I did not understand anything that was said for the entire service. However, the postures—bowing our heads, kneeling, standing, as well as the singing, the smiling, the procession, the energy in the speakers' voices, all communicated the message. Those rituals created a rite that magnified joy. In participating in the liturgy, I was part of something greater than myself. I left the church buoyant with joy and connected to an unexpected community of strangers and to God. Hildegard brought us together to mark a significant time in the continuation of her life story—connecting the present-day saints with the communion of saints across the centuries. This is the power of ritual.

I must add that as I am writing this chapter, I just returned from the solemn feast day Mass of the Passing of Our Holy Father Benedict, Abbot, with the Benedictine monks at St. John's Abbey in Collegeville, Minnesota. Here again, I enter into a ritual that is similar to my own background (Episcopal), but not my own, with strangers gathering to mark the death of St. Benedict—the founder of Hildegard's chosen religious order. I had no idea that it was a special day in the life of the Benedictines, just as before. I feel the significance of each celebration marking time in the birthing of something new in my life. The power of ritual in deepening my connection with Hildegard cannot be ignored.

What is Ritual?

Ritual is a deeply human way of marking significant events and lending a framework to hold and process individual and collective emotion. Think about weddings and funerals. Think about lighting a candle before one prays or meditates. There is preparation, intention, enactment through words and actions, and closing of the ritual time.

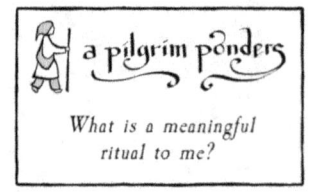

What is a meaningful ritual to me?

Participation in ritual aids in the psychological processing of what our bodies are experiencing. As human beings, we often feel out of control of our circumstances and ritual helps us process those experiences as we give anchors to what might feel overwhelming or ambiguous.

Ritual is especially helpful in finding anchors during the grief process. For example, in my private practice, I will light a candle for someone's loved one who has died and have them bring a picture to put next to it during our session. I have created rituals for people who are struggling with fertility and have had multiple miscarriages so that they may name their hoped-for children and the dreams they had for them. I have done many memorial services for beloved pets, including my own.

While Hildegard would not have put her understanding of ritual in modern terms, she certainly used it and understood its effectiveness in healing.

Ritual and Similar Terms: Some Definitions

People often use and confuse ritual with other terms like routine and rite. Here is a quick look at definitions.

Ritual:[1] (noun) a religious or solemn ceremony consisting of a series of actions performed according to a prescribed order; a series of actions or type of behavior regularly and invariably followed by someone.
— (adjective) relating to or done as a religious or solemn rite;
— (of an action) arising from convention or habit.
— From the Latin: *ritualis, ritus* (rite)
— Examples: bowing, genuflecting (making the sign of the cross), lighting a candle before praying, standing or kneeling at certain times, etc.

Rite:[2] (noun) a religious or other solemn ceremony or act; a social custom, practice, or conventional act. A collection of rituals make up a rite.
— Examples: Sunday worship service, a funeral service, military rites presented at a funeral service, ribbon cutting ceremony, etc.

---

1. *Ritual Meaning*. Definitions from Oxford Languages. Accessed 21 Mar. 2025.
2. *Rite Meaning*. Definitions from Oxford Languages. Accessed 21 Mar. 2025.

Danae Ashley, M.Div., M.A., LMFT

If the difference between rite and ritual is a little confusing, think of it this way: a rite is an established, well-structured and ceremonial act; while rituals are the actions that are performed in a rite with a symbolic meaning.[3] For a visual: Think of the rite as a chalice or wine glass and the rituals as the wine that goes inside the cup—different blends and mixtures that symbolize the maker of the wine, the terroir, etc. A further example is the rite of coronation for those who have monarchs or inauguration for those who have elected officials—there is always a way it is done with rituals within it.

Routine:[4] (noun) a sequence of actions regularly followed; a fixed program.
 — (adjective) performed as part of a regular procedure rather than for a special reason.
 — late 17th century (denoting a regular course or procedure): from French, from route 'road'.
 — Examples: A workout routine; a dog walking routine; a bedtime routine.

Superstition:[5] (noun) excessively credulous belief in and reverence for supernatural beings; a widely held but unjustified belief in supernatural causation leading to certain consequences of an action or event, or a practice based on such a belief.
 — Middle English: from Old French, or from Latin *superstitio(n-)*, from *super-* 'over' + *stare* 'to stand' (perhaps from the notion of 'standing over' something in awe).

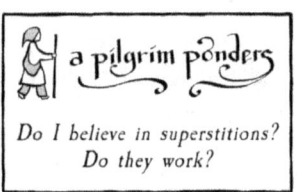
Do I believe in superstitions? Do they work?

 — Examples: In Germany, to wish someone a 'Happy Birthday'

---

3. "Rituals and Rites of Passage in Society | Overview & Examples - Lesson." *Study.Com*, https://study.com/academy/lesson/rituals-rites-of-passage-in-society.html. Accessed 21 Mar. 2025.
4. *Routine Meaning*. Definitions from Oxford Languages. Accessed 21 Mar. 2025.
5. *Superstition Meaning*. Definitions from Oxford Languages. Accessed 21 Mar. 2025.

before their birthday will bring them a year of bad luck. Here's one we're familiar with in North America, too, "Knock on wood." In Germany, this saying refers to the sturdy oak tables that people would sit around for an informal meet-up (*Stammtisch*). Whenever someone joins the table, you give a loud knock on the table. Besides being a robust greeting, this was once a way to ward off the devil. The tables were usually oak, and legend says the Devil can't touch oak so knocking on it proved you weren't the devil. Hildegard would approve!

These definitions are helpful when we read Hildegard's prescriptions for healing, especially what might be true religious ritual and what was medieval superstition.

Recipes, Miracles, and Exorcism, oh my!

Hildegard's holistic approach to healing always began with a person's own connection to God—the Living Light, including the healer's connection. Embodying Virtues instead of Vices was part of self-awareness in moving toward healing. Self-examination continues to be part of modern psychotherapy today. Building on this spiritual foundation, looking at personality temperament and our social context are the next parts of this holistic process. Finally, a prognosis and treatment reflecting everything the healer has learned about the patient is given, often in the form of recipes. This is where the slow medicine takes place—the wait and see, the fine-tuning of the plant in the garden.

Recipes

Hildegard often used recipes for dealing with mental health and spiritual issues which included using herbs, other earthly elements, and/or gemstones in a certain way and then reciting a prayer or other religious incantation to rid the person of the ailment or the evil spirit creating it. She believed in the power of the Earth's elements and the interconnectedness of all creation, which was made by the most powerful element of all: God.

Here are some examples of recipes combining elements from nature, ritual, and prayer:

> *If a person is in the power of an evil spirit, another person should place a sapphire on some earth, then sew that earth into a leather sack, and hang it from his neck. He should say, "O you, most wicked spirit, quickly go from this person, just as, in your first fall, the glory of your splendor very quickly fell from you." The evil spirit will be greatly tortured. He will depart from that person, who will be better, unless it is a very cruel and most good-for-nothing spirit.*[6]

> *If the devil should incite a man to love a woman so that, without magic or invocations of demons, he begins to be insane with this love, and if this is an annoyance to the woman, she should pour a bit of wine over a sapphire three times and each time say, "I pour this wine, in its ardent powers, over you; just as God drew off your splendor, wayward angel, so may you draw away from me the lust of this ardent man." If the woman is unwilling to do this, then another person for whom that love is a problem should do it for her. He should give the wine to the man to drink for three or more days, whether he's eating or not, and whether he knows about it or not. If a woman burns with love for some man, and this is an annoyance to the man, he should do the same thing with the sapphire and the wine, and the burning passion will go away.*[7]

---

6. Hildegard of Bingen. Trans. Throop, Priscilla. *Causes and Cures of Hildegard of Bingen*. 2nd ed., MedievalMS, 2012, 143.

7. Hildegard of Bingen. *Hildegard von Bingen's Physica: The Complete English Translation of Her Classic Work on Health and Healing*. Translated by Priscilla Throop, 2nd ed., Healing Arts Press, 1998, 143.

My Sap is Rising

If someone is bewitched by delusions or magic words, so that he is becoming crazy, take warm rye bread, and cut the shape of the cross in the top crust, not breaking it totally. Drawing a jacinth down through the cut, say, "May God, who threw off every precious stone from the devil when the devil contravened his command, now throw off from you, N., every delusion and all magic words; and may he free you from the pain of this madness." *Then, drawing the same stone across the warm bread, say,* "Just as the splendor which the devil had in him was taken from him because of his transgression, so also let this madness which torments you, N., by various delusions and magic words, be taken from you, and disappear." *The bread from around the area through which you drew the jacinth should be given to the afflicted person to eat. If he cannot eat the rye bread because of the debility of his body, then, using the jacinth and the same words, bless warm, unleavened bread in the same way, and give it to him to eat. In addition, draw the same shape of the cross through all foods which he will eat, namely through meats, vegetable purees, and the rest of his food. If you frequently make crosses on them and bless them with those words, he will be cured. One who has pain in his heart should make the sign of the cross over his heart and say the same words, and he will be better.*[8]

For a person possessed by the devil, pour water over chrysoprase, and say, "O water, I pour you over this stone in that power by which God made the sun as well as the hastening moon." *Give that water as a drink to the one possessed, in whatever way you are able, since he will be unwilling to drink it. For a whole day the devil will be tortured within him, will become weaker, and will not be able to manifest his powers in him, as he had done before. Do this for five days. On the fifth day prepare a bit of bread, with the*

---

8. Hildegard of Bingen. *Hildegard von Bingen's Physica: The Complete English Translation of Her Classic Work on Health and Healing.* Translated by Priscilla Throop, First Edition, Healing Arts Press, 1998, 139-140.

Danae Ashley, M.Div., M.A., LMFT

> *same water poured over it, and give it to him to eat in whatever way you can. If the demon is not fierce, he will depart from that person.*[9]

As you can see from these examples, there is a fair bit of keeping the Devil at bay in Hildegard's time, as well as rite and ritual that seem superstitious. However, might the placebo effect also be in play?

The Mind is a Powerful Thing

Sue Cannon has a persuasive argument in *Hildegard of Bingen Holistic Health Visionary: Twelfth-Century Medical Theories with Modern-Day Appeal* about the placebo effect regarding the cures that Hildegard used. We do not know if any of Hildegard's remedies healed anyone, except for stories about her miracles and exorcisms, so it is unclear what the placebo response was for anyone who came to her for treatment—certainly not in the way that modern science would measure.

The difference between the placebo effect and the placebo response should be clarified for the purpose of this section's discussion. The word 'placebo' means 'I shall be acceptable or pleasing' in Latin, originating from 'placere' (to please). The placebo effect is the difference between being treated with a placebo versus no treatment at all. The placebo response is the measured improvement of a patient's symptoms after being treated with the placebo.[10] Recent neuroscience has studied the placebo response in mice and discovered that the brain does not just light up in the places previously assumed. "They show that the expectation of pain relief is mediated by a population of neurons in a part of the brain's limbic system, a system well established to be involved in pain. Unexpectedly,

---

9. Ibid., 148.
10. Kirsch, Irving. "The Placebo Effect Revisited: Lessons Learned to Date." *Complementary Therapies in Medicine*, vol. 21, no. 2, June 2013, 102–04. *EBSCOhost*, https://doi.org/10.1016/j.ctim.2012.12.003. (accessed 23 March 2025).

however, these neurons send signals to parts of the brainstem and cerebellum. This is a big surprise, given that these regions are usually associated with more-basic functions, such as coordinating movement."[11]

Psychologically, people often experience what they expect to experience. Psychologist and Harvard Medical School researcher Dr. Irving Kirsch explains it this way:

> Various researchers have attempted to assess the magnitude of placebo responses and effects. (1, 2) [12] The underlying assumption of these discussions is that there is a single placebo effect, the magnitude of which can be determined. In fact, there are multiple placebo effects, and their magnitudes depend on a variety of factors. They depend, for example, on the condition being treated. Substantial placebo effects have been found in the treatment of depression and irritable bowel syndrome, (3, 4) but not for infertility, bacterial infections, the common cold, hyperglycemia, cervical dilatation, or marital discord, all of which were included in meta-analytic assessments of the placebo effect. (5)

---

11. Mogil, Jeffrey S. "Placebo Effect Involves Unexpected Brain Regions." *Nature*, vol. 632, no. 8027, Aug. 2024, 990–91. *www.nature.com*, https://doi.org/10.1038/d41586-024-02373-x.

12. Kirsch's footnotes are as follows:

   1. Beecher HK. The powerful placebo. Journal of the American Medical Association 1955;159 (December (17)):1602—6.

   2. Hróbjartsson A, Gøtzsche PC. Is the placebo powerless? Update of a systematic review with 52 new randomized trials comparing placebo with no treatment. Journal of Internal Medicine 2004; 256:91—100.

   3. Kirsch I, Sapirstein G. Listening to Prozac but hearing placebo: a meta-analysis of antidepressant medication. Prevention and Treatment 1998;1(Article 0002a) http://psycnet.apa.org/journals/pre/1/2/2a/ [accessed 26.06.98].

   4. Kaptchuk TJ, Kelley JM, Conboy LA, Davis RB, Kerr CE, Jacobson EE, et al. Components of the placebo effect: a randomized controlled trial in irritable bowel syndrome. British Medical Journal 2008; 336:998—1003.

   5. Hróbjartsson A, Gøtzsche PC. An analysis of clinical trials comparing placebo with no treatment. New England Journal of Medicine 2001; 344:1594—602.

Danae Ashley, M.Div., M.A., LMFT

In a similar vein, Sue Cannon quotes medical philosopher, Lawrence Foss, with what he calls the 'organic solution':

> According to Foss, because humans have the capacity for reflexive, autonomic responses and reflective responses, the patient can "intentionally alter the interior environment in which disease grows" (180). In other words, since we can consider options and outcomes, we can choose a course of action or belief. Beliefs are organized ideas that are assigned meaning and informed by symbols. Beliefs and other cognitive-affective states have a direct causal influence on the generation and course of an ailment. These cognitive-affective states, along with genetics, biochemistry, and environmental vectors together provide the conditions that allow for a patient's vulnerabilities to disease and responses to that disease.[13]

In psychotherapy, we use various methods to alter the cognitive state, such as the talk therapies Dialectical Behavior Therapy (DBT) and Cognitive Behavioral Therapy (CBT), for our thoughts to lead to behaviors and beliefs with the outcome of an overall sense of well-being in our body and mind. While not rituals, some of the skills could be used in creating a ritual for healing.

DBT focuses on helping people accept the reality of their lives and their behaviors, as well as helping them learn to change their lives, including their unhelpful behaviors. DBT was developed in the 1970s by Marsha Linehan, an American psychologist. Typical techniques are: mindfulness, group therapy, pros and cons of a situation, self-soothing, daily affirmation mantras (like the Saturday Night Live's character Stuart Smalley's tongue-in-cheek version of "I'm good enough, I'm smart enough, and doggone it, people like me"), checking the facts, and opposite action (do the opposite of

---

13. Cannon, Sue. *Hildegard of Bingen Holistic Health Visionary: Twelfth-Century Medical Theories with Modern-Day Appeal.* Independently published, 2023, 121.

what your emotions are doing—instead of running away, look them in the eye and speak with confidence—aka "Fake it 'til you make it"). DBT is especially effective for those who feel emotions intensely and have trouble self-regulating.[14]

CBT is a goal-oriented type of talk therapy that is structured and often has a limited number of sessions. It can help manage mental health conditions, such as depression and anxiety, and emotional concerns, such as coping with grief or stress. CBT can also help manage non-psychological health conditions, such as insomnia and chronic pain. Typical techniques are: journaling, breath work (connecting body and mind), using Socratic questioning ("What's the worst that can happen? What would happen if you didn't believe that?"), reframing a situation, and intentional exposure.[15]

Hildegard would never have called any of her healing methods by our modern names, but, in a way, some of what she did is similar to these psychotherapy approaches. However, modern medicine has debunked many of her medieval medicine recipes. Whether her methods worked—placebo response or not—we have no way of measuring because "a similar reduction in symptoms can be produced by the natural progression of a disease, or by the statistical tendency for patients to recover over time."[16]

This brings us to the most important healing factor of all (aside from the Divine): the ministry of presence. As a priest and therapist for almost two decades, I have witnessed countless situations where showing up and sitting with someone in their pain made an immediate difference. Think about how having a parent or other

---

14. "Dialectical Behavior Therapy (DBT): What It Is & Purpose." *Cleveland Clinic*, https://my.clevelandclinic.org/health/treatments/22838-dialectical-behavior-therapy-dbt. Accessed 23 Mar. 2025.
15. "Cognitive Behavioral Therapy (CBT): What It Is & Techniques." *Cleveland Clinic*, https://my.clevelandclinic.org/health/treatments/21208-cognitive-behavioral-therapy-cbt. Accessed 23 Mar. 2025.
16. Mogil, Jeffrey S. "Placebo Effect Involves Unexpected Brain Regions." *Nature*, vol. 632, no. 8027, Aug. 2024, 990–91. *www.nature.com*, https://doi.org/10.1038/d41586-024-02373-x.

trusted adult be present to you when you were hurting made a difference in how quickly you felt better and ready to play again.

When have I given the ministry of presence to another? When have I received it?

Or how a good friend came alongside you when you received difficult news. The ministry of presence matters.

From a spiritual perspective this makes sense. God created us to be in relationship with one another. Jesus sent his disciples out two-by-two. Even if we do not particularly like people, we were created for relationship, connecting to the whole cosmos, but especially other humans.

Anthropologist Daniel E. Moerman researched this phenomenon specifically regarding psychotherapy approaches which resulted in his excellent article entitled "Anthropology of Symbolic Healing" in 1979. In it he finds:

> One recent study reviewed the results of over 100 other studies which compared the effectiveness of various psychotherapeutic techniques. Most of the 100 studies found insignificant differences in the proportions of patients who were improved by various therapies. The form of therapeutic technique used did not seem to change the fact that a high proportion of patients were helped by the psychotherapy. There are only a very few exceptions to the rule that, as yet, patients may be assigned to different treatment techniques at random without affecting the outcome (Luborsky, Singer, and Luborsky 1975).[17]

---

17. Moerman, Daniel E., et al. "Anthropology of Symbolic Healing [and Comments and Reply]." *Current Anthropology*, vol. 20, no. 1, 1979, 59–80.

These findings are further confirmed by Kirsch:

> Data from a study conducted by members of the Program in Placebo Studies (PiPS) show the benefit of taking the time to engender an enhanced therapeutic encounter. (4)[18] We randomized patients suffering from irritable bowel syndrome to either a wait list control condition, placebo treatment with a standard medical interview conducted by a neutral clinician, or the same placebo treatment with an enhanced interview, in which the clinician took the time to listen and express empathy toward the patient and confidence in the treatment. The standard placebo treatment was more effective than doing nothing at all, but the enhanced placebo was significantly more effective.[19]

Clearly the common denominator present in the more successful therapies and placebo treatments was the relationship with the therapist or healthcare provider. Science is finally catching up to what humans inherently know: the ministry of presence is real, and it heals.

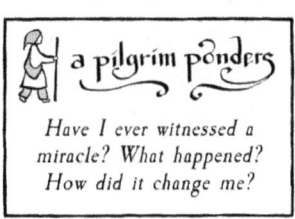

a pilgrim ponders

Have I ever witnessed a miracle? What happened? How did it change me?

Miracles and Exorcism

Miracles were a common way to try to receive healing when people had tried everything else. Many saints and their relics were known to have healing powers, Hildegard included. Like other

---

18. Kirsch's Footnote 4: Kaptchuk TJ, Kelley JM, Conboy LA, Davis RB, Kerr CE, Jacobson EE, et al. Components of the placebo effect: a randomized controlled trial in irritable bowel syndrome. British Medical Journal 2008; 336:998—1003.

19. Kirsch, Irving. "The Placebo Effect Revisited: Lessons Learned to Date." *Complementary Therapies in Medicine*, vol. 21, no. 2, June 2013, 102–04. EBSCOhost, https://doi.org/10.1016/j.ctim.2012.12.003. (accessed 23 March 2025).

saints, she did not even need to be wholly present, as we see from this mental health example in her *Vita*:

> It was of little avail that two women from Staudernheim suffering from emotional illness were taken by their parents to holy places because nothing came of the efforts. But as soon as the nuns laid particles of Hildegard's hair on them, they immediately regained their emotional and bodily health.[20]

In addition to performing miracles, Hildegard was called on to give advice about exorcism rites, as well as perform them with the help of priests, her nuns, and the wider community. According to her *Vita*, there are several examples of this happening:

> A woman, so it was said, was violently distressed by a dumb spirit. The brothers of Laach had for some time been concerned about her. With great effort, some men put her in bed. With trust in the words inspired in her by the Holy Spirit, the good mother [Hildegard] withstood the daring and insolence of the demon, and prayed and blessed her without stopping until by the grace of God the woman was freed from the evil enemy.
>
> In a similar way, she ordered him to leave another woman who, because of her outburst of madness due to her mental illness, was brought to Hildegard bound in chains. To the astonishment of all present, she immediately regained her health of mind and body and with gratefulness went back home.
>
> In the cloister at Aschaffenburg (Schefeneburch) there was a sister whom the devil incited to holy works, prayers,

---

20. Fuhrkkotter, Adelgundis and Mary Palmquist. *The Life of the Holy Hildegard*. Edited by John Kulas, Complete Numbers Starting with 1, 1st Ed edition, Liturgical Pr, 1995, 79.

vigils, and fasting as well as to the reception of the sacraments. Deceitfully, he presented himself as an angel of light. He even tried to upset her by causing her to abhor the names and appearance of certain people and animals of various kinds so that she broke into hours-long howling when she saw and heard them. She was sent to the holy virgin with a letter of recommendation from the prior and the convent and was strengthened by Hildegard and freed from the shrieks of the devil.[21]

Hildegard, through the power of God, was able to cast out demons, just as Jesus' disciples were, and restore each person back to their community and life. What a relief it must have been to each person touched by Hildegard's extraordinary healing through her miracles and exorcisms. No matter what we believe in modern times about demonic possession or mental illness, to return to life in body, mind, and soul, through whatever means, would have been priceless.

---

21. Ibid., 98.

Danae Ashley, M.Div., M.A., LMFT

Pilgrim's Reflection

1. Dr. Bruce Perry, author of the trauma-informed work *What Happened to You?* asserts that "The roots of health are rhythm and regulation." This is precisely what ritual helps us do: have a predictable rhythm in order to regulate. When has ritual been healing in your life?

2. Take a few moments to think about and jot down rituals that you may already be doing during the day, week, or month. How are they working for you in this current season?

3. Create a ritual for this season of life. Ritual is a living tradition, meaning that it can change to fit the needs of the time and season of life. In creating a new ritual, here are some questions to reflect on:

- When I get still within myself, what longing bubbles up?
- What do I truly have energy for? In order for a ritual to be sustainable, we must be honest about what we are capable of doing in this season.
- 'Ease' is the key word for this ritual. Take stock around your house: What do you have at hand that could be used?
- Suggestions: candles, flowers, plants, water, altar/small table, pictures, salt, tea/coffee, food, ribbons/string/twine, rocks, etc.
- How much time do you need?
- How frequently do you want to do this? Daily? Weekly? Monthly?
- Do you need to leave your home to do this? Factor that time in.
- Do you need accountability? If so, what kind? A friend? A calendar task reminder?

4. Have you ever received healing from a placebo? Or have you ever utilized your mind to have a positive outcome in healing? Reflect on those times and write down or make marks on a page about all the different ways you felt supported during that healing time.

Danae Ashley, M.Div., M.A., LMFT

Benediction

This is an inspiring benediction by Hildegard with a commission at the end about the soul that Renate Craine includes in her book *Hildegard: Prophet of the Cosmic Christ*.

> The soul is like a wind that waves over herbs,
> Is like the dew that moistens the grass
> Is like the rain-soaked air that lets things grow.
>
> In the same way you should radiate kindness
> To all who are filled with longing.
>
> Be a wind helping those in need.
>
> Be a dew, consoling the abandoned.
> Be the rain-soaked air, giving heart to the weary,
> Filling their hunger with instruction
> By giving them your soul.

Heilkunde 306[22]

---

22. Craine, Renate. *Hildegard: Prophet of the Cosmic Christ*. Crossroad, 1997, 83.

Group/embodied option: Sit or stand in a circle. As you do the movements, begin with one person saying the first line and the person to their right saying the next, and so on.

(Pat your thighs rapidly, creating the sound of wind or rain)
The soul is like a wind that waves over herbs,
Is like the dew that moistens the grass
Is like the rain-soaked air that lets things grow.

(Place both hands over your heart
and move them out and in like a heart beating.)
In the same way you should radiate kindness
To all who are filled with longing.

(Give yourself a hug, moving your arms
a little out and back in at a steady pace,
ending in time with the last line and a firm hug.)
Be a wind, helping those in need.
Be a dew, consoling the abandoned.
Be the rain-soaked air, giving heart to the weary,
Filling their hunger with instruction
By giving them your soul.

Danae Ashley, M.Div., M.A., LMFT

The soul is like a wind that waves over herbs,
Is like the dew that moistens the grass,
Is like the rain-soaked air that lets things grow.

In the same way, you should radiate kindness,
To all who are filled with longing.

Be a wind, helping those in need.
Be a dew, consoling the abandoned.
Be the rain-soaked air, giving heart to the weary,
Filling their hunger with instruction by giving them...

...your soul.

Chapter 7
There is No Mental Health Without Community

When my congregation's leadership decided to balance the church's budget by eliminating my position almost immediately, it was devastating. They reassured me that it was not personal, my ministry was excellent, and everyone would miss me. But the way it was done (poorly) sure felt personal. It also hurt the congregation, who had already been through other recent communal traumas and were counting on me to be a safe and pastoral presence throughout their transitions.

Upon receiving the news, I activated my personal community to pray for me and for the congregation. Shock, outrage, and prayer poured in. Sadly, this is not the first time a female priest has been treated badly. I have received sexual comments, assumptions about my body, ageism in roles where my leadership and skills were not respected, and many unwanted and unasked-for opinions about my body, sermons, voice, and overall style—often in the greeting line after a church service. I am not alone and I know that others have had it much, much worse. I have heard harrowing tales from female colleagues across denominations including sexual assault, stalking, and being so disrespected and gaslit that they questioned their own call from God. We band together in a multitude of ways as we seek to follow God's call amid microaggressions and personal threats. So, when my community was activated, they showed up.

I floated the idea of going on the pilgrimage to my Women's Wisdom Circle—a small group of faithful women friends I formed in 2018 because I was longing to have deep conversations with other women—and they were immediately onboard. One of them texted our group thread and said that if I created a GoFundMe, that would probably be the easiest way for everyone to donate. I agreed and created a campaign entitled "When the church hurts you, friends will heal you!" I sent it to those beloved women and a dozen or so select others—surpassing my modest goal within a week. The outpouring of encouragement, care, and understanding cocooned me in a soft and shining light of healing as I made my way through Hildegard's land.

Exorcism as a Healing Rite

Alfred Adler's concept of our behaviors being socially embedded and our longing to feel safety, significance, and belonging means that we cannot have good mental health without community. When we are cast outside from a group, it is devastating. Shunning, bullying, and various forms of 'othering' have dire consequences to emotional health. There is a reason that whenever Jesus healed someone, they were always restored to their community—true healing could not happen without this element.

In the medieval period, the ability to perform an exorcism was key for those saints who wished to emulate Christ. Francis of Assisi, Bernard of Clairvaux, Norbert of Xanten, and of course, Hildegard of Bingen, all were known for performing exorcisms.[1] But how much of this was the need for the saint to establish their holiness, compared to what might have been what we would now

---

1. Forcén, Carlos Espí, and Fernando Espí Forcén. "Demonic Possessions and Mental Illness: Discussion of Selected Cases in Late Medieval Hagiographical Literature." *Early Science and Medicine*, vol. 19, no. 3, 2014, 258–79.

call a mental illness or a true demon possession? While not as frequently as for the first reason (sainthood), this is something we continue to assess in modern times. For example, Stefano Ferracuti, Robert Sacco, and Renato Lazzari did a research study regarding Dissociative Trance Disorder (DTD)[2] with ten persons who were going through the exorcism process. They recruited participants for the study by contacting the exorcist of Rome and attending over 400 exorcism rituals for over 100 people, as well as doing psychological testing with ten people who behaved as if they might have DTD.[3]

Exorcism as a healing rite is conducted like other types of religious services with various prayers and actions ordered in a particular way and enacted by a community. The healing power of God is the focus mediated by the religious leaders who lead each ritual within the rite. Ritual actions include prayers, proclaiming Scripture, anointing with oil, laying on of hands, directly commanding the spirit to come out of the person, and giving communion. In my Episcopal tradition, if we suspect a person or place to be possessed in some way, we take this very seriously. In our *Book of Occasional Services*, we are instructed to contact the Diocesan Bishop and they will put us in touch with the Diocesan Exorcist. This person is not known to the public, unlike those saints who performed exorcisms in medieval times. Exorcisms are performed as a last resort after we have exhausted our spiritual and mental health resources.[4]

Interestingly, there are still mild exorcism elements in the vows of the Episcopal baptismal rite. The main purposes of baptism are to bring a person into new life in Christ and into the wider

---

2. The *Diagnostic and Statistical Manual of Mental Disorders*, 5th edition, text revision *(DSM-V-TR)* calls this Other Specified Dissociative Disorder (OSDD).
3. Ferracuti, Stefano, and Roberto Sacco. "Dissociative Trance Disorder: Clinical and Rorschach Findings in Ten Persons Reporting Demon Possession and Treated by Exorcism." *Journal of Personality Assessment*, vol. 66, no. 3, June 1996, 525. EBSCOhost, https://doi.org/10.1207/s15327752jpa6603_4.
4. https://www.episcopalchurch.org/glossary/exorcism/

Christian community, which requires a change of life that is focused on God's ways, eschewing the ways of sin. These exorcism elements include rituals such as the 'Questions and Answers' litany (Do you renounce Satan and all the spiritual forces of wickedness that rebel against God? *I renounce them.*)[5] and making the sign of the cross on the person's forehead with blessed chrism oil (in early Christian times it was the oil of exorcism) while proclaiming *"Name of person,* you are sealed by the Holy Spirit in Baptism and marked as Christ's own forever."[6]

No matter if a person is suffering from a mental illness or possessed, exorcism is a healing rite. The purpose is to restore the person to health and community, in hopes that they will stay well.[7] Hildegard gave us a detailed description of one such exorcism that she performed while at Rupertsberg.

Case Study: The Exorcism of Lady Sigewize

In 1169, Hildegard had been ill for some time when she received a letter from Gedolphus, Abbot of Brauweiler, who knew Hildegard only by reputation, about a young noblewoman who was possessed by a demon for eight years. The Abbot tried to liberate her for three months and failed. Finally, the demon cried out that it could only be cast out by "the strength of your [Hildegard's] contemplation and the magnitude of divine revelation."[8] A rather put upon Hildegard responds to Abbot Gedophus' letter with a long, rather complicated rite for exorcism:

---

5. Church Publishing Inc. *Book of Common Prayer, Pew, Red.* Pew edition, Church Publishing, 1979, 302.
6. Ibid., 308.
7. While this chapter is focused on healing and community, if you would like a comprehensive reflection on possession and mental illness, Carlos and Fernando Espí Forcén have an excellent exploration in their article "Demonic Possessions and Mental Illness: Discussion of Selected Cases in Late Medieval Hagiographical Literature." *Early Science and Medicine,* vol. 19, no. 3, 2014, 258–79.
8. Baird, Joseph L., editor. *The Personal Correspondence of Hildegard of Bingen.* 1st edition, Oxford University Press, 2006, 80.

> *Although I have been confined with a long and serious illness through the scourges of God, I have just enough strength to answer your request. What I am about to say does not come from myself, but from the One Who Is...*
>
> *...Hear, then, the answer, not of a human being but of the One Who Lives. Choose seven priests of good repute, recommended by the quality of their life, in the name and order of Abel, Noah, Abraham, Melchisedech, Jacob, and Aaron, for these offered sacrifice to the living God. The seventh priest will represent Christ, who offered his very self on the cross to God the Father. And with fasting, scourges, prayers, and oblations, let them celebrate Mass, and, then, clad in their priestly vestments and stoles, let them approach around her, each one holding a rod in his hand in figure of that rod with which Moses struck Egypt, the Red Sea, and the rock at God's command [Ex. 7.9-10.23; 14.16-29; 17.6], so that, just as there, God revealed his miracles through the rod, so also, here, He may glorify Himself when that foul enemy has been cast out through these rods...*[9]

And so on and so forth until the priests begin striking the woman lightly and saying,

> *"Now, you, O satanic and evil spirit, you who oppress and torment this person, this form of a woman, depart! Through Him Who lives and Who has revealed these words through a simple person untaught in human learning, leave this person who is here present and whom you have oppressed for a long time, and in whom you still remain. For you have been commanded, and He Himself now commands you to begone. And so by this rod at the command of the True Beginning, that is, the Beginning Itself, you are commanded to harm her no further. Conjured and condemned*

---

9. Baird, Joseph L., editor. *The Personal Correspondence of Hildegard of Bingen.* 1st edition, Oxford University Press, 2006, 80-81.

also by the sacrifice and prayers and aid of Abel, in whose name we strike you."[10]

With other declarations in the same vein.

Gedolphus writes that the exorcism was unsuccessful and tells Hildegard he is sending the Lady Sigewize directly to her at Mount St. Rupert for exorcism and healing. In Hildegard's *Vita*, Theoderic of Echternach writes even more details from a lost document of Hildegard's:

> "Meanwhile," Theoderic writes, citing Hildegard herself, "I was informed that in the lower parts of the Rhine, at some distance from us, there was a certain noble woman possessed by the devil. I heard about her frequently. And I saw in a true vision that, by the permission of God, she had been possessed and overshadowed by a smoky black, demonic glob, which oppressed all the sensibilities of her rational spirit and did not allow her to sigh out to God in her proper senses, just as smoke or the shadow of man or an object obscures and envelops. Hence she had lost all her normal faculties and actions, and frequently shouted out indecent things and acted in improper ways. But sometimes she was less oppressed when, by God's command, this torment diminished somewhat..."[11]

Hildegard said of Sigewize's arrival,

> "We were shocked about the news of the woman since that meant we had to see and hear the lady who had upset people for so long a time. But God trickled the dew of his sweetness down on us. And without fear and alarm and without human help we brought her here to the living quarters of the sisters. In spite of the horror and

---

10. Ibid., 82.
11. Baird, op. cit., 87.

the disturbance with which the demon frightened all those nearby...we did not give up on our part."[12]

Later, Hildegard receives a letter from the dean at The Holy Apostles in Cologne, telling her that he heard that she cast the demon out of the noble woman, Sigewize, who was a good friend. Hildegard downplays her role in her return letter. Instead, she points to God, but also gives us a moving outline of how the entire community—convent and village and beyond—assisted in Sigewize's healing:

On her [Sigewize's] behalf, the exalted, and the even more exalted, the lowly, and even more lowly, have spoken as one with their labors and prayers, and have clamored as individuals, in accordance with the instructions of the Holy Spirit. For some individuals have labored on her behalf through sighs of compassion; others, by prayers and vigils; and others, by fasts and scourgings. Moreover, many have given alms for her sake, and a large number of others have taken her part by helping her with all the good in their power. Others have brought this duty to completion with their great and persistent zeal. Thus, just as the day completes its cycle, all were looking to God at the time for her sake.[13]

Between Hildegard's *Vita* and her letters referencing the exorcism of Lady Sigewize, we have a fairly full understanding of Hildegard's approach. Of course, in any hagiography, the saint's holy traits are highlighted and often sensationalized. However, the information in her letters is enough even without the more salacious details that Theoderic reveals in the *Vita*.

This exorcism and subsequent healing are what we will explore

---

12. Fuhrkkotter, Adelgundis, and Mary Palmquist. *The Life of the Holy Hildegard*. Edited by John Kulas, Complete Numbers Starting with 1, 1st edition, Liturgical Pr., 1995, 86.
13. Baird, Joseph L., editor. *The Personal Correspondence of Hildegard of Bingen*. 1st edition, Oxford University Press, 2006, 86.

in more detail regarding how vital community participation was for its success, reiterating again that we cannot have good mental health without community.

What can we learn from this case study?

Suzanne M. Phillips and Monique D. Boivin's insightful article "Medieval Holism: Hildegard of Bingen on Mental Disorder" explores Sigewize's treatment to showcase support for Hildegard's holistic thinking especially in light of being healed through embedded social context (as Adler would say).[14] The following is their outline:

> Hildegard's response to Sigewize's[15] arrival is instructive. She took this troubled woman into her cloistered community and provided her with wide-ranging care.
>
> (1) Sigewiza was taken into the living quarters of the abbey's nurse.
>
> (2) She always had a sister of the community at her side to share in her sufferings with empathy.
>
> (3) She was incorporated into the daily routines of the religious community, including mealtimes, prayers, and the giving of alms.
>
> (4) Hildegard also spoke continually with the spirit possessing Sigewiza, persistently identifying the demonic presence within the woman.
>
> (5) Furthermore, the surrounding community became involved in seeking Sigewiza's healing through prayer and the giving of offerings to the church (Phillips & Boivin, 360-361).

---

14. Phillips, Suzanne M., and Monique D. Boivin. "Medieval Holism: Hildegard of Bingen on Mental Disorder." *Philosophy, Psychiatry, & Psychology*, vol. 14, no. 4, 2007, 359–68.
15. This is a different translation of Sigewize's name and not a misspelling. I have kept it because it is a direct quote from the article.

Note on (5) from *The Life of the Holy Hildegard*: "For that reason, we and the men and women of our village, from the feast of the Purification of Mary [February 2] until the Saturday before Easter, busied ourselves with prayers, alms, and bodily penance for the woman" (94).

(6) When the people of the region gathered for the Festival of Maria, they were told that Sigewiza would be healed forty days later, on the day before Easter. The forty days were a time of preparation for the healing, during which many people in the community combined their efforts to assist Sigewiza.

(7) An exorcism was finally conducted on the day before Easter, and this time it was successful (Schipperges 1985, 62).[16]

This outline is compelling in clearly seeing the way the community had a vital part in Sigewize's healing. "The roots of health are rhythm and regulation," Dr. Bruce D. Perry wrote in his collaborative book with Oprah Winfrey *What Happened to You?: Conversations on Trauma, Resilience, and Healing*.[17] We have already discussed the importance of ritual in a person's life and for Sigewize, being part of the daily rituals which created the rhythms of the abbey would have given her a predictable schedule (Benedictines pray the hours[18]), in addition to participating (as much as she could) in the Benedictine integration of moderation in prayer and work, as well as rest. With rhythm established, regulation could occur. Studies have shown that human beings need to be able to self-regulate and co-regulate their parasympathetic systems.[19]

---

16. Phillips, Suzanne M., and Monique D. Boivin. "Medieval Holism: Hildegard of Bingen on Mental Disorder." *Philosophy, Psychiatry, & Psychology*, vol. 14, no. 4, 2007, 361.
17. Perry, Bruce D. and Oprah Winfrey. *What Happened to You?: Conversations on Trauma, Resilience, and Healing*. 1st edition, Flatiron Books: An Oprah Book, 2021.
18. Benedict of Nursia. *The Rule of Saint Benedict: A Contemporary Paraphrase*. Edited by Jonathan Wilson-Hartgrove, Paraclete Press, 2012, 39.
19. Porter, Chris L., et al. "Development of Mother-Infant Co-Regulation: The Role of

Danae Ashley, M.Div., M.A., LMFT

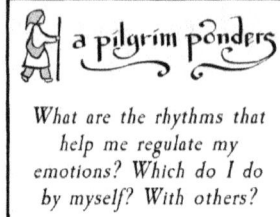

What are the rhythms that help me regulate my emotions? Which do I do by myself? With others?

When we have trouble regulating imbalance within ourselves alone, we need others to step in. We need ways to be reminded that we are not alone, we are created in God's image, our brokenness did not happen in isolation, nor will it be healed in isolation, and we are worthy of respect and dignity just by existing. The sociobiological systems that are part of a religious community activate psychological, sociological, and physical responses in us.[20] In Sigewize's story and our own, these ways of being in community make healing become a way of life instead of a one-time event.

Infant Vagal Tone and Temperament at 6, 9, and 12 Months of Age." *Infant Behavior and Development*, vol. 67, May 2022, 101708. *ScienceDirect*, https://doi.org/10.1016/j.infbeh.2022.101708.

20. Alarcón, Renato D., and Julia B. Frank. *The Psychotherapy of Hope: The Legacy of Persuasion and Healing*. Johns Hopkins University Press, 2012. *ProQuest Ebook Central*, http://ebookcentral.proquest.com/lib/csbsju/detail.action?docID=3318756.

Pilgrim's Reflection

1. When have you been faced with unexpected circumstances that required you to 'activate' your network of support? Was it difficult to ask for help? Reflect on these questions and also how it feels when someone you care about is going through a difficult time and you want to help, but they refuse or do not ask.

2. Make a list of who is part of your community. Make a commitment to write a letter or send a card of appreciation to each person or organization over the course of two years.

3. Whether or not you believe evil spirits are real, Lady Sigewize was clearly suffering. What did you find interesting in the case study of Lady Sigewize? Are there parts of Hildegard's holistic approach that you think would be helpful in today's time?

4. What would it be like if we had systems in place to care for those suffering from mental illness like Hildegard and her community cared for Sigewize? Is there one thing you can do to care for your distressed neighbors?

Danae Ashley, M.Div., M.A., LMFT

Benediction

Renowned Hildegard historian Barbara Newman translates Hildegard's flowery, often excessive writing, brilliantly maintaining the core spirit with contemporary language. Here is Hildegard's "Sequence for the Holy Spirit"[21] which is also a blessing for all those in need of encouragement.

> Fiery Spirit,
> fount of courage,
> life within life
> of all that has being!
>
> Holy are you, transmuting the perfect
>   into the real.
> Holy are you, healing
>   the mortally stricken.
> Holy are you, cleansing
>   the stench of wounds.
>
> O sacred breath O blazing
> love O savor in the breast and balm
> flooding the heart with
> the fragrance of good,
>
> O limpid mirror of God
> who leads wanderers
> home and hunts out the lost,
>
> Armor of the heart and hope
> of the integral body,

---

21. Hildegard of Bingen. *Symphonia: A Critical Edition of the "Symphonia Armonie Celestium Revelationum."* Translated by Barbara Newman, Cornell University Press, 1998, 149-151.

sword-belt of honor:
save those who know bliss!

Guard those the fiend holds
Imprisoned,
free those in fetters
whom divine force wishes to save.

O current of power permeating all
in the heights upon the earth and
in all deeps:
you bind and gather
all people together.

Out of you clouds
come streaming, winds
take wing from you, dashing
rain against stone;
and ever-fresh springs
well from you, washing
the evergreen globe.

O teach of those who know,
a joy to the wise
is the breath of Sophia.

Praise then be yours!
you are the song of praise,
the delight of life,
a hope and a potent honor
granting garlands of light.

Danae Ashley, M.Div., M.A., LMFT

Group option: Have one person read the stanzas meditatively, but with energy and joy, while the others partner up and form a circle around them. The partner on the left is 1 and the partner on the right is 2. If there are not enough people to have an even number, the extra person can join the person in the middle and they can take turns reading the stanzas. Follow the directions in *italics* echoing the movement of the Holy Spirit.

(1)
(Hold hands in the circle and walk toward the middle, raising arms.
Then walk back, lowering arms but still holding hands.)
Fiery Spirit,
fount of courage,
life within life of all that has being!

(2)
(Circle to the left.)
Holy are you, transmuting the perfectinto the real.
Holy are you, healing
the mortally stricken.
Holy are you, cleansing
the stench of wounds.

(3)
(Circle to the right.)
O sacred breath O blazing
love O savor in the breast and balm
flooding the heart with
the fragrance of good,

My Sap is Rising

(4)
(Grand Chain for Stanzas 4-6: Turn to face your partner.
*Take right hands count **one** (in your head) and go past,*
*hold out left hand to next person count **two** and go past, etc.*
Partner 1 goes anticlockwise; Partner 2 goes clockwise.
You do not stay with your partner
*but keep moving and counting until you get to **seven**.*
Once you get to seven, face the middle of the circle
and hold hands with your new partner.)
O limpid mirror of God
who leads wanderers
Home and hunts out the lost,

(5)
Armor of the heart and hope
of the integral body,
sword-belt of honor:
save those who know bliss!

(6)
Guard those the fiend holds
Imprisoned,
free those in fetters
whom divine force wishes to save.

(7)
(Partner 1s walk forward toward the middle of the circle,
raising their arms and wiggling their fingers,
then walk back lowering their arms.)
O current of power permeating all
in the heights upon the earth and
in all deeps:
you bind and gather
all people together.

Danae Ashley, M.Div., M.A., LMFT

(8)
(Partner 2s walk forward toward the middle of the circle, raising their arms and wiggling their fingers, then walk back lowering their arms.)
Out of you clouds
come streaming, winds
take wing from you, dashing
rain against stone;
and ever-fresh springs
well from you, washing
the evergreen globe.

(9)
(Everyone takes a deep breath.)
O teach of those who know, a joy to the wise
is the breath of Sophia.

(10)
(Hold hands in the circle and walk toward the middle, raising arms. Then walk back, lowering arms but still holding hands. Drop hands and spin once with arms in the air.)
Praise then be yours!
you are the song of praise, the delight of life,
a hope and a potent honor
granting garlands of light.

Symphonia 28

 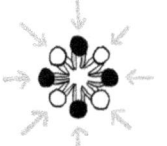 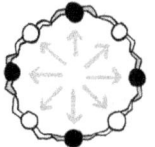

Fiery Spirit,   *life within life*   *of all that has being!*
fount of courage,

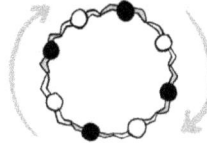 

Holy are you, transmuting   *O sacred breath!*
the perfect into the real.   *O blazing love!*
Holy are you, healing   *O savor in the breast*
the mortally stricken.   *and balm flooding the heart*
Holy are you, cleansing   *with the fragrance of God!*
the stench of wounds.

O limpid mirror of God, who leads wanderers home and hunts out the lost
Armor of the heart and hope of the integral body, sword belt of honor,
Save those who know bliss!
Guard those the fiend has imprisoned,
Free those in fetters whom divine force wishes to save!

Danae Ashley, M.Div., M.A., LMFT

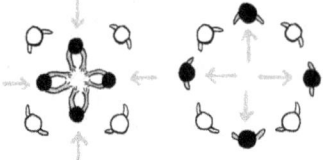 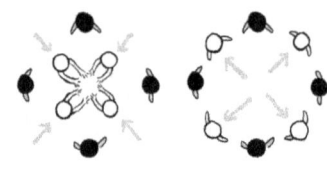

O current of power permeating all, in the heights upon the earth and in all deeps, you bind and gather all people together.

Out of you clouds come streaming, winds take wing from you, washing the evergreen globe.

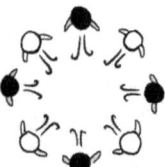

O teach of those who know, a joy to the wise is the breath of Sophia.

 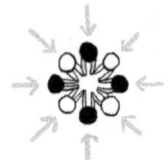 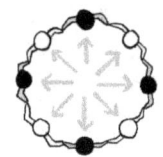

Praise then be yours!

You are the song of praise, the delight of life,

a hope and a potent honor...

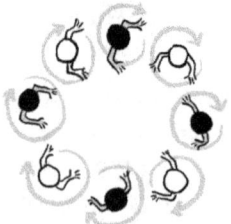

...granting garlands of light.

Chapter 8
Embodied Creativity in Healing

I listened to the bright birdsong of the morning as I made my way on the gravel path underneath a canopy of trees, rich in various hues of green that were glinting in the sunlight. It was the Feast Day of the Ascension, and I was meeting a couple who were fellow pilgrims, Christian and Alice, at the Chapel of St. Roch,[1] down the road from where we were staying at the Hildegard Forum in Bingen. We met at breakfast and got to talking, as one does on pilgrimage, and discovering we were both doing the Hildegard Way. They were German and had talked to the sexton (caretaker) of St. Roch's, making an appointment with him to get a tour of the inside of the building, and invited me along.

I couldn't believe my luck. I had tried to enter St. Roch's when I arrived the day before, but it was locked. You could enter the main doors to light a candle at a prayer station and peek into the nave, but there were black iron gates preventing further entry. What I learned from Alice and Christian was that there were two sites in Bingen that had Hildegard relics and St. Roch's was one of them. I could not wait to see the reliquary. The other site was the Parish Church of St. Rupertus and St. Hildegard in the heart of Bingen and

---

1. I love St. Roch. He is the patron saint of dogs!

Danae Ashley, M.Div., M.A., LMFT

I was going to walk down to see it later that day on my way to the Museum am Strom on the banks of the Rhine. Christian explained to me that Ascension Day was a holiday in Germany so all the museums and other cultural sites would be open. I prayed that the Holy Spirit and Hildegard continued guiding my steps because I was going to try my luck at seeing the remaining vaults of the Rupertsberg monastery, which was closed when I had tried the day before.

St. Roch's is big. And pink. Well, pink and white like a birthday cake. It is a delicious Gothic-style church that was finished being built in 1895 and was designed by a prominent church architect at the time, Max Meckel. This was the third iteration of the chapel after the others had been destroyed (the latest in 1889), including almost all the furnishings that came from the dissolution of the convent of Eibingen in 1814. There were only a few paintings and the relics of St. Hildegard, St. Rupertus, St. Berta, and St. Wigbert that were rescued. However, in honor of the connection to St. Hildegard, Margarethe Krug donated a lavish Hildegard altar based on an imitation of one of the rescued pictures showing Hildegard's life. It is there that her small reliquary sits snugly below a central half-relief statue of Hildegard with various scenes of her life on either side.[2] According to tradition, one of Hildegard's ribs and a piece of her habit reside there. Soaking in the artwork about her life and her presence was powerful.

It seemed like no matter where I went on my pilgrimage, Hildegard inspired all sorts of creativity, just as she was creative

---

2. Rath, Philippa, et al. *Hildegard of Bingen: Historical Sites*. 3rd edition, Schnell & Steiner, 2014.

My Sap is Rising

herself. I saw multiple renditions of her and her life in paintings, prints, mosaics, gardens, churches, museums, sculptures, and statues. *Viriditas* blazed in all of them. Hildegard was such an embodied person—never leaving out the body from the experiences of the mind and spirit—that it is not surprising that her legacy is embodied, too.

Visual Art

The illuminations of Hildegard's *Scivias* visions are stunning and strange. A quick search on the internet will bring up her most popular ones such as "The Visionary" (one of my favorites)—a picture of Hildegard receiving her visions from a fiery flame into the top of her head as she writes them down with her loyal helper, the monk Volmar, looking into the room. This sets the stage for *Scivias* and describes Hildegard's experience of receiving this vision in her 43rd year of life: "A fiery light came down from the open sky with flashes. It flowed through my brain and glowed through my heart and chest like a flame." Hildegard scholar Sr. Maura Zátonyi, OSB explains more about the illuminations: We do not know if Hildegard or Volmar or other nuns created these illuminations to capture Hildegard's visions. The Abbey of St. Hildegard says this about the pictures' origins:

> The 35 miniatures have contributed significantly to the fame of the Liber "Scivias", the first vision script of Hildegard von Bingen. These pictures are found in the so-called illuminated magnificent manuscript and are perhaps more popular than the written text of the work itself. There are no definitive

research results on the arising and essence of the miniatures. The dating period of the manuscript is generally recognized during Hildegard's lifetime, i.e. before 1179. The Rupertsberg Monastery as a place of origin also seems undisputed. Although the original manuscript of the Scivias Codex has been lost since 1945—for security reasons itwas moved from the Nassau State Library Wiesbaden to Dresden shortly before the end of the war—we have a valuable facsimile thanks to the meticulous work of our sisters who faithfully copied the manuscript by hand in 1927-1933. Naturally, something of vitality and originality was lost in the fine repainting of the pictures. Nevertheless, this facsimile gives an accurate impression of the original, especially as regards the variety of colors (translated from German). [3]

Another popular image is the mandala-style "Choir of Angels"[4] —a depiction of nine angel choirs surrounding a blank white circle in the middle: the mystery of God. Sr. Maura Zátonyi OSB writes:

The angelic choirs "resound in every kind of music and proclaim in miraculous harmonies the miracles that God works in holy souls – a song of glorification of God" (Scivias I.6.11). The concentric circles condense around the great mystery of God, which the pure spirits are already allowed to look [at] and whose vision people long for. The middle of the miniature, to which the great round dance of the angelic beings moves, is white—God's mystery is veiled, because

---

3. *Die „Scivias"-Miniaturen – BENEDIKTINERINNENABTEI ST. HILDEGARD.* 9 Dec. 2011, https://abtei-st-hildegard.de/die-scivias-miniaturen/. Accessed 4/12/2025.
4. 'Choir of Angels' Fol 038 of the Rupertsberg Scivias Codex of Saint Hildegard of Bingen, around 1175, original lost since 1945, hand copy on parchment 1930, Abbey of St. Hildegard, Rüdesheim-Eibingen.

"as long as man is mortal, he cannot fully recognize the eternal" (Scivias I.6.10.).[5]

One of Hildegard's early depictions of the cosmos that is also one of my favorites is often called the 'Cosmic Egg'. It is translated as "The Space" on the Abbey of St. Hildegard website and represents God's activity in creation in Hildegard's third vision. [6]

It, too, is a mandala-style drawing, but in an oval shape instead of the round. There are very clearly feminine elements in its construction: it is shaped like a vulva with inner and outer lips, a vaginal opening in the center with the urethra opening directly above it, and a clitoris made from a red star or flower at the top. It is "interpreted in a symbolic sense by the divine voice in the course of the vision. In this way we learn to spell out the universe towards

---

5. *"Scivias"-Code: Panel 9: The Choirs of the Angels – BENEDIC SECTORS ST. HILDE-GARD.* https://abtei-st-hildegard.de/%e2%80%9cscivias%e2%80%9d-kodex-tafel-9-die-chore-der-engel/. Accessed 26 Mar. 2025.
6. 'The Space/Cosmic Egg' Fol 014 of the Rupertsberg Scivias Codex of Saint Hildegard of Bingen, around 1175, original lost since 1945, hand copy on parchment 1930, Abbey of St. Hildegard, Rüdesheim-Eibingen.

the content of the faith."[7] As Hildegard says in this vision, "Not only the visible and temporal makes God known through his creation, but also the invisible and eternal" (Scivias I.3.1.).

I have cards of each of these illuminations on my desk because they capture my imagination with their bold colors and the meaning behind each vision. They remind me of the definition of Jesus' parables that I learned in seminary from the writings of British scholar C.H. Dodd: "At its simplest, a parable is a metaphor or simile, drawn from nature or the common life, arresting the hearer by its vividness or strangeness, and leaving the mind in sufficient doubt about its precise application to tease it into active thought."[8] This is what the portrayal of Hildegard's visions do for me. Her descriptions are copious, but the artist's interpretations lend themselves to the "vividness or strangeness" that Dodd talks about, teasing the mind into active thought. Hildegard's images are compelling, especially paired with her strange and wondrous visions to deepen the meanings.

Praying with Hildegard's Illuminations

Hildegard's illuminations are also like icons, and I sometimes use them as such. If you have never prayed with an icon and do not know what I am talking about, please let me explain. A Christian icon is a two-dimensional depiction of Jesus, Mary, angels, saints,

---

7. *"Scivias"-Code: Panel 4: The Universe – BENEDICAT RESULT ST. HILDEGARD.* https://abtei-st-hildegard.de/%e2%80%9cscivias%e2%80%9d-kodex-tafel-4-das-weltall/. Accessed 26 Mar. 2025.
8. Brosend, William. *Conversations with Scripture - The Parables.* Morehouse Publishing, 2006, 11.

or other significant holy figures that is "written" (painted) traditionally on wood with intention and prayer. The purpose is not to have a realistic image like a portrait, but a stylized symbolic one. The faces are static, and the colors symbolize important Christian theology, such as gold representing the radiance of Heaven, blue as human life, and red as Divine life. This tradition comes out of early Christianity and the Eastern Orthodox churches, but many across the world find the spiritual practice of writing an icon edifying and take classes from master iconographers to learn the craft. There are also contemporary (mainly Western) iconographers who are more flexible with the tradition than the Orthodox.

So, you may be saying to yourself, it is nice that people like to paint pictures of holy people and turn them into icons, but how do you use it if you are not the one creating it? Icons are used for prayer—they are windows into the divine. You pray by simply looking at them and seeing what draws your eye, meditating on whatever it is that draws you as you invite God to speak to you. After a time, you can thank God for the gift of resting in God's presence and close your prayer time. You can do this with a traditional icon or something like one of Hildegard's images, which have much symbolism and directly speak about God's work in the world.

Mandalas and Prayer

Mandala means "circle" in Sanskrit and is used in Buddhist and Christian meditation. The circle is also a Biblical symbol (Ezekiel 1) and appears in everything from the Celtic cross to cathedral rose windows. Carl Jung wrote of it as a universal symbol of wholeness. I am a trained Mandala Assessment Research Institute (MARI) facilitator which explores the common mandala archetypes and relates them to a person's life cycle and symbols in a mandala of

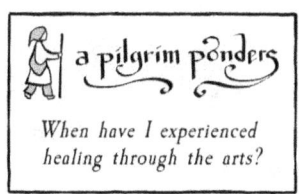

When have I experienced healing through the arts?

their creation. Mandalas are everywhere, including in Hildegard's visionary work as I mentioned above.

There are a number of ways to create a mandala. You may have witnessed or watched a video of Zen Buddhist monks creating elaborate sand mandalas only to sweep them away when they were finished. For them, it is used for meditation and to remind the person of the universe and impermanence of the world. Hildegard created mandalas to reflect what she saw in her visions. They, too, represented certain aspects of the universe—like the choir of angels or creation—and can be used for meditation with her writings. There are also coloring books of mandalas that you can fill in if you do not want to create your own.

I use mandalas in my therapy practice and spiritual direction frequently. I have my clients create their own. The circle of the mandala represents a safe place in which to express oneself: safe from the inner critic and safe for things that might be big and frightening (like grief or anger) to emerge or be expressed. When used this way, the mandala is a sanctuary of wholeness and healing, a way of letting our inner selves be expressed in a context of healing and prayer.

The Healing Power of Singing Together

There is an old saying that church choir members always enjoy sharing: *When you sing, you pray twice.* Hildegard grew up singing the psalms with Jutta, singing Mass, and hearing music in her visions. As a composer, she brought these auditory visions to life in her own hymns, the *Ordo Virtutum*, and other compositions. She took the opening of Psalm 100 "Make a joyful noise to the Lord, all ye lands" seriously.

Shortly before her death, when Hildegard and her nuns were under interdict for burying an excommunicated young man in consecrated ground, the most difficult part was not being denied communion, but not being able to sing the divine office. Hildegard was sure the man had reconciled with the church before he died, and fought to restore her convent, but it took a lot of pleading and finally getting witnesses to say that he had reconciled with the church before he died to get the archbishopric of Mainz to lift the interdict. A selection from her letter to the prelates of Mainz articulates her passion for music and her theology for its use:

> *By a vision, which was implanted in my soul by God the Great Artisan before I was born, I have been compelled to write these things because of the interdict by which our superiors have bound us, on account of a certain dead man buried at our monastery, a man buried without any objection, with his own priest officiating. Yet only a few days after his burial, these men ordered us to remove him from our cemetery. Seized by no small terror, as a result, I looked as usual to the True Light, and, with wakeful eyes, I saw in my spirit that if this man were disinterred in accordance with their commands, a terrible and lamentable danger would come upon us like a dark cloud before a threatening thunderstorm...*
>
> *...Therefore, you and all prelates must exercise the greatest vigilance to clear the air by full and thorough discussion of the justification for such actions before your verdict closes the mouth of any church singing praises to God or suspends it from handling or receiving the divine sacraments. And you must be especially certain that you are drawn to this action out of zeal for God's justice, rather than out of indignation, unjust emotions, or a desire for revenge, and you must always be on your guard not to be circumvented in your decisions by Satan, who drove humanity from celestial harmony and the delights of paradise.*
>
> *Consider, too, that just as the body of Jesus Christ was born of the purity of the Virgin Mary through the operation of the Holy Spirit so, too, the canticle of praise, reflecting celestial harmony, is rooted in the Church through the Holy Spirit. The body is the vestment of the spirit, which has a living voice, and so it is proper for the body, in harmony with the soul, to use its voice to sing praises to God....*
>
> *...And because sometimes a person sighs and groans at the*

> sound of singing, remembering, as it were, the nature of celestial harmony, the prophet, aware that the soul is symphonic and thoughtfully reflecting on the profound nature of the spirit, urges us in the psalm [cf. Psalm 32:2] to confess to the Lord with the harp and to sing a psalm to Him with the ten-stringed psaltery. His meaning is that the harp, which is plucked from below, relates to the discipline of the body; the psaltery, which is plucked from above, pertains to the exertion of the spirit; the ten chords, to the fulfillment of the law.
>
> Therefore, those who, without just cause impose silence on a church and prohibit the singing of God's praises and those who have on earth unjustly despoiled God of honour and glory will lose their place among the chorus of angels, unless they have amended their lives through true penitence and humble restitution...[9]

Hildegard believed singing was a divine activity which connected the singer with the angels and the cosmos. She knew it was vital for her community and saw how they all suffered without it. Psychologically, there have been multiple studies about how singing with a group improves mental health and overall well-being. It is a social act as well as physical; the whole body is involved when one sings. Singing in groups is something that humans are inclined to do across cultures and across time.

Singing is healing. Polyvagal theory uses singing and humming to help regulate the nervous system. Remember Dr. Perry's quote: "The roots of health are rhythm and regulation"? That is what singing does. Dr. Cathy Malchiodi explains how it works this way:

> In particular, the ventral vagal network that runs from the diaphragm to the brain stem is key because it can be influenced by breathing patterns and social cues such as smiling and making eye contact to generate a sense of calm and

---

9. Baird, Joseph L., editor. *The Personal Correspondence of Hildegard of Bingen*. 1st edition, Oxford University Press, 2006, 156-161.

safety. Experiences that generate sounds such as gargling, humming, prosody, and specific vocalizations can also be self-regulatory. These practices can help us find ways to "rest and digest" when hyperactivation or dissociation overtake brain and body.[10]

Although Hildegard could not articulate why singing was vital in today's psychological jargon, she certainly knew how healing it was.

Relic Collecting

After being drawn into awe and wonder at the altar reliquary in St. Hildegard's Parish Church, I came out of my daze and noticed the rest of the space. As you approach the altar, the wall on the left had artful presentations of items in a large display case wrapped in either red or white fabric. When I got closer, I realized that they were bones. Not just any bones, but heads, legs, and arms of various saints with names in Latin that I had never heard: Bertae, Wilperti, and Valeriani. I discovered the arm of St. Rupert, to whom Hildegard had dedicated her monastery at Rupertsberg and who is fittingly the patron saint of pilgrims. There was the head of Bertae which is translated as St. Berta, St. Rupert's mother. She led St. Rupert in her Christian example, and both lived on the hill next to Bingen which became Rupertsberg where they established hospices for those in need in the area. There was also the head of St. Gudula, one of the national saints of Belgium and Patroness of Brussels. These were all part of Hildegard's personal relic collection in which she found inspiration and comfort.

You may be wondering why I would include relic collecting as an embodied practice for healing. Humans have used the body and

---

10. *Tapping the Healing Rhythms of the Vagal Nerve | Psychology Today.* https://www.psychologytoday.com/us/blog/arts-and-health/202004/tapping-the-healing-rhythms-of-the-vagal-nerve. Accessed 27 Mar. 2025.

items that it touched as a bridge between the divine realm and their communities across millennia. From the cult of human skulls in Near Eastern Neolithic people to Egyptian mummies, to Christian saint relics to the contemporary practice of creating a necklace or paperweight out of cremains, humans have a desire to connect to their ancestors and loved ones for wisdom and protection beyond the grave.

This honoring the divinity of the body and our connection to familial and spiritual ancestors supports Hildegard's understanding of the entwining of body and soul. The earliest Christian relic or talisman noted in 384 by the pilgrim Egeria was a letter from Jesus to King Abgar.[11] It had powerful protection for the city of Edessa where it was enshrined. Constantine was also known to have multiple talismans enshrined in his capital such as fragments of the True Cross, and the relics of the apostles Andrew, Luke, and Timothy.[12] These objects were important not only in performing miracles and giving protection, but also in church politics—being bought or sold for power. The medieval period was rife with relics and relic hunters for these reasons.

The relics Hildegard collected clearly captured her imagination by being related to a saint she took personal inspiration from or was related to her work. Having the bone of a saint to intercede on one's behalf and amplify prayers strengthened the connection between the Divine and the person or community. They are also embodied reminders of the communion of saints who have gone before. Psychologically, people are embodied in the physical world and need touchstones to assist them in growth and healing. A relic of any kind can be a touchstone for us as we assign our own meaning to it.

---

11. Wiśniewski, Robert. *The Beginnings of the Cult of Relics*. Oxford University Press, Incorporated, 2019. *ProQuest Ebook Central*, http://ebookcentral.proquest.com/lib/csbsju/detail.action?docID=5606643, 65.
12. Wiśniewski, Robert. *The Beginnings of the Cult of Relics*. Oxford University Press, Incorporated, 2019. *ProQuest Ebook Central*, http://ebookcentral.proquest.com/lib/csbsju/detail.action?docID=5606643, 65.

Drama and Dance

Hildegard's use of drama in the *Ordo Virtutum* and the dance of liturgy—bow, kneel, genuflect, stand, and other postures of prayer—is vital to her experience of God and healing. Dressing up in anything other than their habits to participate in special services drew criticism from other religious leaders. While Hildegard was still at the Disibodenberg, but already the *magistra* of the women's community, she received a letter from Mistress Tengswich outlining her outrage at Hildegard's practices. It begins with praise for Hildegard's "saintliness" and the rumor that she is writing down the "secrets from heaven" (*Scivias* had not been completed yet) and then moves into thinly veiled contempt for the way Hildegard and her nuns are dressing up for certain services:

> We have, however, also heard about certain strange and irregular practices that you countenance. They say that on feast days your virgins stand in the church with unbound hair when singing the psalms and that as part of their dress they wear white, silk veils, so long that they touch the floor. Moreover, it is said that they wear crowns of gold filigree, into which are inserted crosses on both sides and the back, with a figure of the Lamb on the front, and they adorn their fingers with golden rings. And all this despite the express admonition: Let women comport themselves with modesty "not with plaited hair, or gold, or pearls, or costly attire" [I Tim 2.9]...
>
> ...O worthy bride of Christ, such unheard-of practices far exceed the capacity of our weak understanding, and strike us with no little wonder. And although we feeble little women wholeheartedly rejoice with all the esteem due your

spiritual success, we still wish you to inform us on some points relative to this matter...[13]

Hildegard swiftly justifies her practices with a beautiful theology of womanhood, especially for the Middle Ages.

The Living Fountain says: Let a woman remain within her chamber so that she may preserve her modesty, for the serpent breathed the fiery danger of horrible lust into her. Why should she do this? Because the beauty of woman radiated and blazed forth in the primordial root, and in her was formed that chamber in which every creature lies hidden. Why is she so resplendent? For two reasons: on the one hand, because she was created by the finger of God and, on the other, because she was endowed with wondrous beauty. O, woman, what a splendid being you are! For you have set your foundation in the sun, and have conquered the world.

...Listen: The earth keeps the grass green and vital, until winter conquers it. Then winter takes away the beauty of that flower, and the earth covers over its vital force so that it is unable to manifest itself as if it had never withered up, because winter has ravaged it. In a similar manner, a woman, once married, ought not to indulge herself in prideful adornment of hair or person, nor ought she to lift herself up to vanity, wearing a crown and other golden ornaments, except at her husband's pleasure, and even then with moderation.

But these strictures do not apply to a virgin, for she stands in the unsullied purity of paradise, lovely and unwithering, and she always remains in the full vitality of the budding rod...

...These words do not come from a human being but from the Living Light. Let the one who hears see and believe where these words come from.[14]

---

13. Baird, Joseph L., editor. *The Personal Correspondence of Hildegard of Bingen*. 1st edition, Oxford University Press, 2006, 25-26.
14. Baird, Joseph L., editor. *The Personal Correspondence of Hildegard of Bingen*. 1st edition, Oxford University Press, 2006, 26-29.

Hildegard's creativity was one of the many gifts that she used to honor God. It also brought her great pleasure to create dramatic liturgies where she and her nuns would embody roles such as the Virtues. These experiences were rich and meaningful to their relationship with God and brought them closer as a community.

Adlerian Link

Adler recognized each person as "both the picture and the artist."[15] Many Adlerian Art Therapists use art as a way of fostering encouragement, insight, and social interest. The Adlerian approach to therapy lends itself to creativity in crafting meaningful homework for clients and in-session role plays or other kinds of creative engagement. Adler had a high view of artists:

> *In our view, a man of genius is primarily a man of supreme usefulness. If he is an artist, he is useful to culture, giving distinction and value by his work to the recreative life of many thousands. This value, where it is genuine and not merely empty brilliance, depends upon a high degree of courage and social interest.*[16]

In my own practice, I rely on music, drama, dance/movement, and art to help my clients get out of their head and into their heart. I find that the arts are often the best way for the Holy Spirit to assist in swift and deep healing. As I traveled to the different Hildegard pilgrimage sites, I noticed how people were inspired to create because of their experience of Hildegard's work. I saw paintings, drawing, sculptures, and gardens, as well as tasted food and heard music by Hildegard. It was clear that Hildegard tapped into others' *viriditas* across the centuries, and I got to enjoy the fruits of their sap rising, just as mine was growing inside.

---

15. Ansbacher, Heinz L., and Rowena R. Ansbacher, editors. *The Individual Psychology of Alfred Adler: A Systematic Presentation in Selections from His Writings.* Harper Perennial, 1964, 177.
16. Ansbacher & Ansbacher, op. cit., 153.

Danae Ashley, M.Div., M.A., LMFT

Pilgrim's Reflection

1. Which of these practices intrigued you: icon, mandala, singing, relic collecting, or drama and dance? Why? Is there anything blocking you from trying something new?

2. You can create a mandala with what you have on hand. Here are some simple instructions:

- Gather together a piece of paper (scrapbook size is perfect, but any size will do), colors (crayons, cray-pas, pencils, markers), and a candle.
- Light the candle and take deep breaths to quiet your mind.
- With your non-dominant hand, let a color choose you and draw a dinner-plate sized circle on your page (adjust to page size as needed).
- Continuing with your non-dominant hand, let a new color choose you and begin to fill in the space with what feels right. Let new colors choose you as it feels good. The mandala is often abstract, but not always. This is not a performance, this is a process, so please quiet your inner critic.
- When you feel like you are slowing down, ask yourself if there is anything else that needs to be on the page and put that down.
- When you are finished, close your eyes and take a deep breath of gratitude for the time spent.
- Open your eyes and look at your mandala from different angles. The position in which you created it may not be the position from which it needs to be viewed. It will let you know.

- Finally, ask your mandala its name. Write the name in the corner along with the date.
- Blow out or turn off your candle with a final prayer of thanksgiving for this meditative time.

3. We have lost the art of singing together and rely on professionals to do something that is innate to being human. Consider this parable about a young fiddler and a wizard (told best by my fiddler friend, Larry Young):

> There once was a young fiddler who came from a musical family. Everyone played wonderfully...except him. He loved playing the fiddle, but when he practiced, everyone would not only leave the room, but leave the house! Finally, he decided to seek the advice of a great wizard who he heard granted wishes.
>
> After searching high and low, he found the wizard in a pub. After some conversation, the wizard agreed to grant the young lad a wish, but he would have to choose: When he played the fiddle, did he want to sound beautiful to himself or to others? What a choice! What would you choose?
>
> The young fiddler chose to have the music sound beautiful to him. So, he went home, and he began to play. It sounded like the angels from heaven! This made him want to play more and over time, he began to improve. People did not run away from his music any longer and he lived a long, happy life playing the fiddle.

The moral of the story is that even if you feel like you cannot carry a tune in a bucket, God wants you to make a joyful noise. My husband is a professional musician and church choir director, and he reminds me that almost everyone can learn to sing (except the approximately 2% of the population who are medically tone deaf)[17] —it is a skill that you must want to learn. Here are some invitations:

- Sign up for singing lessons or get some coaching from your faith community's music director or other music professional.
- Join a community choir, whether in a sacred or secular setting. When we sing with others, it lessens the anxiety of having your voice being the only one heard. You can learn a lot about the skill of singing, breath support, and reading music in a choir. It also supplies an excellent connection to community, which is helpful for mental health.
- Sing karaoke with friends and family. You can do this in the privacy of your own home with YouTube and a karaoke microphone. There are also places that rent karaoke rooms or you can go to a bar (if you are of age) that hosts karaoke nights. The point is to have fun and enjoy making a joyful noise… again, community for the mental health win!
- Support live music and go to a concert where you can sing at the top of your lungs with hundreds of other fans.

4. How do you honor the dead? How do you keep connection with and receive inspiration from those who have gone before you? Consider creating your own altar of artifacts from people who give you strength on your life journey. This can be in a corner of a room or on a mantle. You may want to include pictures, mementos, prayer cards, candles, or even cremains if you have them. Whatever

---

17. Peretz, Isabelle, and Dominique T. Vuvan. "Prevalence of congenital amusia." *European journal of human genetics : EJHG* vol. 25,5 (2017): 625-630. doi:10.1038/ejhg.2017.15 (accessed 24 July 2025).

you include, make sure that they are talismans that draw you closer to God and to wisdom.

5. Some of the Benedictions in this book are a way to engage in embodied prayer. Are there poems, songs, or other texts that you could make up your own movements to?

Danae Ashley, M.Div., M.A., LMFT

Benediction

God was music to Hildegard and all of creation joins in a glorious song throughout the ages. We can join with Hildegard in this "Antiphon for the Trinity"[18] adding our voices to hers.

Group option: Read this out loud together with strong and joyful voices, as Hildegard and her nuns would have sung it.

> To the Trinity be praise!
> God is music, God is life
> that nurtures every creature in its kind.
> Our God is the song of the angel throng
> and the splendor of secret ways
> hid from all humankind,
> But God our life is the life of all.

Symphonia 26

---

18. Hildegard of Bingen. *Symphonia: A Critical Edition of the "Symphonia Armonie Celestium Revelationum."* Translated by Barbara Newman, Cornell University Press, 1998, 143.

Chapter 9
Hildegard's Own Mental Health

Throughout my pilgrimage, I witnessed the many ways that Hildegard drew people to her. It was as if she was a rock thrown into the pond of life and the weight and substance of her contributions continue to ripple through time. Hildegard has been called many things throughout the centuries: Prophetess (Sibyl of the Rhine), Composer, Physician and Healer (first gynecologist and founder of scientific natural history in Germany), Environmentalist, Preacher (four preaching tours beginning in her 60s), Mystic, Advisor to all social classes, Writer, Linguist of her own alphabet '*Litterae ignotae*' and language '*Lingua ignota*', Visionary, and Christian saint. She is all these things and more.

In the local history museum in Bingen, Museum am Strom (Museum on the River), there is a permanent exhibit on Hildegard, including an outdoor garden with many of the herbs and plants she mentions in her works. People from all over the world learn about this remarkable woman who is included in a long line of polymaths through history. Her exuberance for learning and creative application across diverse fields is astounding for a woman in the twelfth century and is the reason we know about her today.

Danae Ashley, M.Div., M.A., LMFT

Migraines or Neurodiversity or Something Else?

Throughout her writings and across her life, we hear of Hildegard suffering from a variety of things that kept her bedridden for days. There are a number of theories out there—that she had migraines or possibly an autoimmune disorder that was attacking her nervous system or a version of schizophrenia or other diseases that affected her vision and energy. Or could it be that the life of a medieval nun living in poverty in the 12th century was a difficult life and these ailments stem from housing conditions and nutrition issues? Hildegard seemed to have boundless energy in between illness.

It is difficult and sometimes dangerous to diagnose someone from the past, but people are fascinated by Hildegard and have a variety of educated guesses about what was happening to her mentally. Charles Singer and Oliver Sacks[1] both believed that Hildegard suffered from migraines with accompanied phenomena. Peter Harteloh disagrees. He writes:

> …as a medical doctor, I think that her visions cannot be classified as pathological. There are voices accompanying the images. Migraines are not accompanied by voices. According to the DSM-V, the current manual for psychiatric diseases (APA 2022), hearing voices that instruct behavior are a hallmark of schizophrenia and seeing images are a hallmark of delirium. An interweaving of voices and images cannot be classified as a delirium or symptom of schizophrenia. Also, the voices and images are followed by thoughts as reflection on the experience…In the case of Hildegard, visions serve a deeper understanding of the world, the gospel (God's word) and herself. They are transcendental in the sense that the person of Hildegard dissolves in the

---

1. Flanagan, Sabina. *Hildegard of Bingen: A Visionary Life*. 2nd ed., Routledge, 1998, 191.

vision. So, Hildegard's visions are a kind of transcendental meditation rather than pathological phenomena. Medical interpretations should be avoided.²

Annelore Wherthmann posited a psychoanalytic approach to Hildegard's life, and "pointed out several traumatic events in the course of Hildegard's life and discovered the ingredients of a narcissistic coping process. In line with psychoanalytical theory, she explained Hildegard's visions as a withdrawal into a closed inner world."³

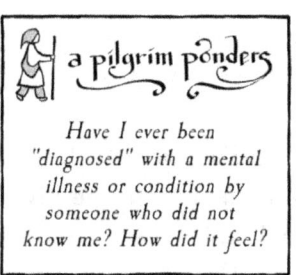

Have I ever been "diagnosed" with a mental illness or condition by someone who did not know me? How did it feel?

The withdrawal into her own world leads us to more recent musings about Hildegard's possible neurodiversity. Patricia Ranft's 2014 article "Ruminations on Hildegard of Bingen (1098-1179) and autism" is careful not to give a diagnosis of being on the autism spectrum but outlines several ways in which Hildegard exemplifies those characteristics. She was a child "beset with an undefined 'weakness', social isolation, deficits in expressive oral communication, difficulty in expressing needs, extreme distress at failed attempts at relationship and withdrawal in the face of failure."⁴ Visual thinking, hyperlexia, special interests, musical mastery, and self-discipline are other characteristics that Ranft highlights.

Building on Ranft's ruminations, Janko Nešić, Vanja Subotić, and Petar Nurkić wonder about the therapeutic role of the monastic

---

2. Harteloh, Peter. "Hildegard of Bingen: Philosophical Life and Spirituality." *Religions*, vol. 15, no. 4, 4, Apr. 2024, 506. *www.mdpi.com*, https://doi.org/10.3390/rel15040506.
3. Ibid.
4. Ranft, Patricia. "Ruminations on Hildegard of Bingen (1098-1179) and Autism." *Journal of Medical Biography*, vol. 22, no. 2, May 2014, 107–15. *PubMed*, https://doi.org/10.1177/0967772013479283.

environment for those on the autism spectrum using Hildegard as a case study.[5] They include Hildegard's development of the *Lingua Ignota* as further evidence of her being an autistic person. They explore how monastic life with its repetition of prayers, daily chores, candlelight, and silent meals seem ideal for a person who experiences sensory overload and anxiety with rapid change. There are concurring arguments that monasteries were just the right place for those who were neurodiverse or did not fit into society, such as Christine Trevett's idea of the Holy Fool and the case of the Franciscan Brother Juniper.[6]

What do you think?

Being a Wounded Healer

I do not know exactly what caused Hildegard's illnesses. But I do know that psychologically, not being in alignment with the Living Light—one's core values and that still, small voice within—causes psychological issues that can turn into physical ailments. As a spiritual person, I believe that Hildegard's visions were from God. As noted in the first chapter, it takes a lot of energy spiritually and physically to be a vessel of the Divine. After the Lady Sigewize's exorcism, Hildegard fell ill for more than forty days. This example, in her words, exemplifies the energy it takes to heal others and supports the idea that when she obeyed the Living Light, her physical ailments improved.

> Soon after the lady was released from her possession, a severe illness [in 1170] again took hold of me, so that both my veins—

---

5. Nešić, Janko, et al. "The Therapeutic Role of the Monastic Environment for Individuals with ASC: The Case of Hildegard of Bingen and Her Lingua Ignota." *Eidos. A Journal for Philosophy of Culture*, vol. 8, no. 2, Aug. 2024, pp. 7–26. doaj.org, https://doi.org/10.14394/eidos.jpc.2024.0008.

6. Trevett, Christine. "Asperger's Syndrome and the Holy Fool: The Case of Brother Juniper." *Journal of Religion, Disability & Health*, vol. 13, no. 2, Dec. 2009, 129–50. EBSCOhost, https://doi.org/10.1080/15228960802581537.

with blood—and my knees—with their marrow—become sluggish, my innards were stirred up, and my entire body was as exhausted as grass that loses its fresh green look in the winter. I saw how the evil spirit sneered at this and with derision said: "Hurrah! This lady is going to die, and her friends, with whom she brought us into confusion, will mourn." However, I saw that the departure of my soul had not yet come. I suffered more than forty days and nights with this illness.

Meanwhile, in a true vision, it was revealed to me that I should search for some cloistered communities of men and women and share with them the words which God had revealed to me. When I finally prepared to do that, although my bodily strength was diminishing, the weakness disappeared somewhat. I revealed the wisdom of God and was able to get rid of some of the discord existing in the cloisters. If, because of fear of the people, I took no notice of the ways shown to me by God, my bodily pains took over and did not leave until I had obeyed. It happened the same way with Jonah who was severely oppressed until he prepared to obey.[7]

Hildegard's incredible ability to heal others may be partially the result of her being what Carl Jung called a 'wounded healer,' meaning that the best healer is one who has their own wounds and understands this in others. Henri Nouwen wrote a book called *Wounded Healer*, identifying Jesus as a wounded healer and sharing how we draw from this archetype in contemporary ministry. Hildegard understood this centuries before Jung and Nouwen, living her life through God's strength in her wounds.

Adlerian Link

What implications does this have for psychotherapists and

---

7. Fuhrkkotter, Adelgundis and Mary Palmquist. *The Life of the Holy Hildegard.* Edited by John Kulas, Complete Numbers Starting with 1, 1st Ed edition, Liturgical Pr, 1995, 95-96.

those in caring professions such as ministry and healthcare? How do we use our own differences and wounds to care for others? What would Adler say?

In my private practice, many of my clients come to me because they know I am an Episcopal priest, and they want to use their spirituality as part of their healing. Sometimes they too have been wounded by the Church or other religious tradition but still feel connected to the Divine and seek help in finding comfort and strength in that connection. Even if a healer does not believe in the Divine themselves, James Griffith notes that "[p]sychotherapy and religion may find common ground in strengthening personal spirituality. From a secular position, a psychotherapist may help a patient find within his or her religious tradition those beliefs, practices, and communal ways of living that best foster coherence, hope, communion, purpose, gratitude, and other existential states."[8]

Wounded healers are also those who, like Hildegard and Adler, have gone through adversity and used various resources to come out the other side. It is powerful to have someone who has been in similar circumstances and is now thriving hold out their hand to bring you up to where they are. This is what Adler talks about when he claims there is no good mental health without community. We all must operate socially on the horizontal axis together and not the vertical axis pushing others down. A wounded healer helps others see why their life matters. Hildegard would say you are God's creation and matter to God; this means that God has meaningful work for you in this life. Adler would say you have significance and belonging just by being a human and this means you are also charged with the responsibility of social interest to encourage others in their journey. No matter what life throws at us, we are not

---

8. Alarcón, Renato D., and Julia B. Frank, Eds. *The Psychotherapy of Hope: The Legacy of Persuasion and Healing.* Johns Hopkins University Press, 2012. *ProQuest Ebook Central,* http://ebookcentral.proquest.com/lib/csbsju/detail.action?docID=3318756, 320.

alone and can use what we have gone through to assist others. But how do wounded healers care for themselves?

As shown in Hildegard's example of healing the Lady Sigewize and in other times of her life when she had visions or was not heeding the Living Light, Hildegard was forced to rest. This is a cautionary tale for those in the healing profession. We must tend to ourselves, or our wounds will overwhelm us. How do we stay open to work the Divine has invited us to do and survive being a vessel of healing? I find this challenging because I like helping others and feel good doing it. Some weeks, I find that I have to say no to interesting and fun projects and new clients because I have overextended myself with the ones I already have. I start getting irritable, feel unfocused, and want to withdraw. That is when I know I need to ingather my energy and discern what God needs me to focus on. If I do not take the time when I notice, my body will force me to take it.

There is no way of truly knowing if Hildegard had a modern diagnosable illness or mental health issue. However, we can certainly learn from her own stories about what she did with what she had, and that is a worthy legacy to follow.

It Is Solved by Walking

I was in a distressed state when I began Hildegard's Way. I was angry, sad, disillusioned, exhausted, overwhelmed, scared, depressed, and lost in many ways. While those feelings did not magically go away over the course of ten days, they certainly lightened. I had a routine comprised of ease: waking up naturally, eating a hearty German breakfast, filling my travel mug with water (it had pictures of my soul dog, Alvie Anne, all over it), getting on the road and driving across beautiful country and into charming villages each day to find the tableaus. I would take food from breakfast for lunch and eat when I was hungry, stopping to take in the views and just be. I had good weather and was thankful for that, too. Each night, I would get to my next *Pension* or hotel before

Danae Ashley, M.Div., M.A., LMFT

dark and either have dinner there or ask where I should eat. I explored local foods and local beers and wines even though I am normally almost a complete teetotaler. I would go back to my lodgings and connect with my community via WhatsApp before planning the next day's journey and downloading the maps to my phone in case I did not have cell service. I drifted off to sleep grateful for this opportunity and excited for the next day.

In this *Kairos* time, some of the raw edges softened. I received clarity and experienced kindness from others which invited me to be kind to myself. My sap began to rise again. I would not feel the fog of grief lift until almost a year after my church released me from my position. I did not have everything healed or figured out by the end of my pilgrimage. I would have loved more time on Hildegard's Way, but this was the time I was given, and I gave myself to it fully, knowing that the healing magic of Hildegard would keep working long after I left her land.

Pilgrim's Reflection

1. Do you have a theory about Hildegard's mental health? If so, what in your own story might you connect with your theory about Hildegard?

2. One of the main techniques in Adler's Individual Psychology is the use of encouragement. Adlerian psychotherapists encourage their clients to distinguish between what they do (behaviors) and who they are (a human being worthy of dignity and respect).

   - Which behaviors that no longer serve you need to be teased out from who you are? List three.
   - Take those three behaviors and reflect on how they have helped you or worked for you in the past. How are they working for you now?
   - Ask yourself "The Question" for each: How would your life look and feel if you woke up tomorrow and no longer had this issue?
   - Journal or reflect in detail about what would be different.
   - Take courage and write one baby step toward the change you need to make for each.

3. We can all identify as wounded healers when we get in touch with our own resilience. Here are some questions to ponder:

   - What helps you endure through difficult times?
   - What gives you hope amid pain?
   - Who else understands what you are experiencing? A person? A group? God?
   - Where do you find comfort when you suffer?
   - What have been glimmers of joy despite illness or difficulties?
   - How do your struggles fit into your story?

Danae Ashley, M.Div., M.A., LMFT

Benediction

Hildegard believed that everything happened according to God's will and saw sinfulness as a way of the Devil getting the Soul off its path. One of four of Hildegard's songs without music, this "Song to the Creator"[9] reminds us that the universe is much larger than we are and God's power encompasses it all.

Group option: Engage in *lectio divina* with this song. This way of studying Scripture and other sacred texts was encouraged by St. Benedict, and Hildegard would have known this form of study as a Benedictine nun. You may do this for individual reflection, as well. Here are the steps:

1. Have one person read the song slowly aloud and then have a quiet minute to reflect on this question: *What word or phrase jumps out at you?* People may want to jot this and other reflections down in a journal or on a piece of paper throughout this exercise. Each member of the group is invited to share without elaboration.
2. Have a second person read the song aloud and give one minute of silence to reflect on this question: *What feelings are invoked for you in this passage?* Each person may share briefly.
3. Have a third person read the song aloud and give two minutes of silence to reflect on this question: *What is God calling me to do from this reflection?* Each person is invited to share and engage in group discussion.

---

9. Hildegard of Bingen. *Symphonia: A Critical Edition of the "Symphonia Armonie Celestium Revelationum."* Translated by Barbara Newman, Cornell University Press, 1998, 259.

You, all-accomplishing
Word of the Father,
are the light of primordial
daybreak over the spheres.
You, the foreknowing
mind of divinity,
foresaw all your works
as you willed them,
your prescience hidden
in the heart of your power,
your power like a wheel around the world,
whose circling never began
and never slides to an end.

Symphonia Song to the Creator

Chapter 10
Final Thoughts

On my last morning at the Hildegard Forum in Bingen, I had a final robust German breakfast with Alice and Christian. It was bittersweet saying goodbye to my new friends. They were going on to their next pilgrimage destination and my pilgrimage was essentially over. I wondered what would sink in from my experience, what would have a profound influence, and what I would forget. I definitely wanted to integrate those breakfasts into my daily routine, as well as more walking. I knew I was coming back changed in other ways but did not know how.

I am still discovering ways that Hildegard's ripple effects are reaching my life. My hope is that you have been changed by the echo of Hildegard's influence through this work and that you have also found inspiration for healing in the brief doses of Alfred Adler. Whether you used this book for your own personal journey or with a group, I pray that your sap also rises and you are moved to continue your own pilgrimage way as a feather on the breath of God.

Danae Ashley, M.Div., M.A., LMFT

Pilgrim's Reflection

1. What are your main takeaways from this pilgrimage through psychotherapy with Hildegard and Adler?

2. How would you describe this book to someone else?

3. What are two things you will try from this book in your life moving forward?

Benediction

A final Benediction from Hildegard's *Book of Life's Merits*, paraphrased by Carmen Acevedo Butcher. [1] May we each be a "zither of love" in the world.

Group option: Divide into two groups. Group One read '1' and Group Two read '2.' When finished, discuss what it would look like for you to become a "zither of love."

(1) Heaven's my home, and God's love is my desire.
(2) I will seek to yearn for my Creator above all things.
(1) My greatest wish is to do what You ask me, God.
(2) Give me wings of determination and kindness,
(1) so I can soar above the stars of heaven,
(2) doing Your good will.
(1) You and Your holiness are all I need.
(2) Make me Your zither of love!

---

1. Butcher, Carmen Acevedo. *Hildegard of Bingen, Doctor of the Church: A Spiritual Reader*. Paraclete Press, 2013, 147-148.

Works Cited

Akbari, Suzanne Conklin, and Jill Ross. *The Ends of the Body: Identity and Community in Medieval Culture*. University of Toronto Press, 2013. *ProQuest Ebook Central*, http://ebookcentral.proquest.com/lib/csbsju/detail.action?docID=4670064.

Alarcón, Renato D., and Julia B. Frank. *The Psychotherapy of Hope: The Legacy of Persuasion and Healing*. Johns Hopkins University Press, 2012. *ProQuest Ebook Central*, http://ebookcentral.proquest.com/lib/csbsju/detail.action?docID=3318756.

Alexiu, Andra. "Demon Possessed or Spirit-Filled? Religious Dissent and Feminine Religiosity in the Twelfth Century Rhineland." *I Quaderni Del m.æ.s. - Journal of Mediæ Ætatis Sodalicium*, vol. 22, no. 1s, June 2024, pp. 141–63. *maes.unibo.it*, https://doi.org/10.6092/issn.2533-2325/19075.

American Psychiatric Association. *Diagnostic and Statistical Manual of Mental Disorders, Text Revision Dsm-5-Tr*. 5th edition, Amer Psychiatric Pub Inc, 2022.

Ansbacher, Heinz L., and Rowena R. Ansbacher, editors. *The Individual Psychology of Alfred Adler: A Systematic Presentation in Selections from His Writings*. Harper Perennial, 1964.

Armstrong-Carter, Emma, et al. "Self-regulated Behavior and Parent-child Co-regulation Are Associated with Young Children's Physiological Response to Receiving Critical Adult Feedback." *Social Development*, vol. 30, no. 3, Aug. 2021, pp. 730–47. *EBSCOhost*, https://doi.org/10.1111/sode.12498.

Aronson, Jeff. "When I Use a Word... Please, Please Me." *BMJ: British Medical Journal*, vol. 318, no. 7185, 1999, pp. 716.

Askeland, Harald, et al. *Understanding Values Work: Institutional Perspectives in Organizations and Leadership*. Springer International Publishing AG, 2020. *ProQuest Ebook Central*, http://ebookcentral.proquest.com/lib/csbsju/detail.action?docID=6112021.

Attridge, Harold W., and Society of Biblical Literature. *HarperCollins Study Bible: Fully Revised & Updated*. HarperOne, 2006.

Baert, Barbara, et al. *Disembodied Heads in Medieval and Early Modern Culture*. BRILL, 2013. *ProQuest Ebook Central*, http://ebookcentral.proquest.com/lib/csbsju/detail.action?docID=1357632.

Baird, Joseph L., editor. *The Personal Correspondence of Hildegard of Bingen*. 1st ed., Oxford University Press, 2006.

"Behaviors in Men That Could Be Signs of Depression." *Mayo Clinic*, https://www.mayoclinic.org/diseases-conditions/depression/in-depth/male-depression/art-20046216. Accessed 19 Mar. 2025.

Benedict of Nursia. *The Rule of Saint Benedict: A Contemporary Paraphrase* edited by Jonathan Wilson-Hartgrove, Paraclete Press, 2012.

Works Cited

Bobzien, Alli. "Jagged Edges and All." *America Magazine: The Jesuit Review of Faith & Culture*, vol. 232, no. 2, Feb. 2025, pp. 56–57.

Boivin, Monique D. and Phillips, Suzanne M. "Medieval Holism: Hildegard of Bingen on Mental Disorder." *Philosophy, Psychiatry, & Psychology*, vol. 14, no. 4, 2007, pp. 359–68.

Boyce-Tillman, June. "Music and Well-Being." *The Journal for Transdisciplinary Research in Southern Africa*, vol. 10, no. 2, 2, Nov. 2014, p. 22. *td-sa.net*, https://doi.org/10.4102/td.v10i2.96.

Brosend, William. *Conversations with Scripture - The Parables*. Morehouse Publishing, 2006.

Brown, Brené. *The Gifts of Imperfection: 10th Anniversary Edition: Features a New Foreword and Brand-New Tools*. Anniversary edition, Hazelden Publishing, 2022.

Brown, Walter A. "The Placebo Effect." *Scientific American*, vol. 278, no. 1, 1998, pp. 90–95.

Bruscia, Kenneth. *Case Studies in Music Therapy*. Barcelona Publishers, 1991. *ProQuest Ebook Central*, http://ebookcentral.proquest.com/lib/csbsju/detail.action?docID=4617333.

Buckley, Peter. "Mystical Experience and Schizophrenia." *Schizophrenia Bulletin*, vol. 7, no. 3, Jan. 1981, pp. 516–21. *EBSCOhost*, https://doi.org/10.1093/schbul/7.3.516.

Butcher, Carmen Acevedo. *Hildegard of Bingen, Doctor of the Church: A Spiritual Reader*. Paraclete Press, 2013, 147-148.

Cannon, Sue. *Hildegard of Bingen Holistic Health Visionary: Twelfth-Century Medical Theories with Modern-Day Appeal*. Independently published, 2023.

Cedeno, Rommy, and Tyler J. Torrico. "Adlerian Therapy." *StatPearls*, StatPearls Publishing, 2025. *PubMed*, http://www.ncbi.nlm.nih.gov/books/NBK599518/.

Church Publishing Incorporated. *Book of Common Prayer, Pew, Red*. Pew edition, Church Publishing, 1979.

Cilliers, L. and Retief, F. P. "The Influence of Christianity on Graeco-Roman Medicine Up to the Renaissance." *Akroterion*, vol. 46, 2001. *akroterion.journals.ac.za*, https://doi.org/10.7445/46-0-120.

Clarke, Kris, and Michael Yellow Bird. *Decolonizing Pathways Towards Integrative Healing in Social Work*. Taylor & Francis Group, 2020. *ProQuest Ebook Central*, http://ebookcentral.proquest.com/lib/csbsju/detail.action?docID=7245245.

"Cognitive Behavioral Therapy (CBT): What It Is & Techniques." *Cleveland Clinic*, https://my.clevelandclinic.org/health/treatments/21208-cognitive-behavioral-therapy-cbt. Accessed 23 Mar. 2025.

Coon, Lynda L. "The Beginnings of the Cult of Relics." *Church History*, vol. 89, no. 4, Dec. 2020, pp. 908–09. *EBSCOhost*, https://doi.org/10.1017/s0009640721000147.

Craine, Renate. *Hildegard: Prophet of the Cosmic Christ*. Crossroad, 1997.

Davidson, Audrey Ekdahl. *The Ordo Virtutum of Hildegard of Bingen: Critical Studies*. Medieval Institute Publications, 1992.

De Ruddere, Lies, et al. "Health Care Professionals' Reactions to Patient Pain: Impact of Knowledge About Medical Evidence and Psychosocial Influences." *The Journal*

Works Cited

of Pain, vol. 15, no. 3, Mar. 2014, pp. 262–70. DOI.org (Crossref), https://doi.org/10.1016/j.jpain.2013.11.002.

"Dialectical Behavior Therapy (DBT): What It Is & Purpose." *Cleveland Clinic*, https://my.clevelandclinic.org/health/treatments/22838-dialectical-behavior-therapy-dbt. Accessed 23 Mar. 2025.

Die „Scivias"-Miniaturen – BENEDIKTINERINNENABTEI ST. HILDEGARD. 9 Dec. 2011, https://abtei-st-hildegard.de/die-scivias-miniaturen/.

Drazenovich, George, and Celia Kourie. "Mysticism and Mental Health: A Critical Dialogue." *HTS Teologiese Studies / Theological Studies*, vol. 66, no. 2, 2, Sept. 2010, p. 8.

Dronke, Peter, editor. *Nine Medieval Latin Plays*. Cambridge University Press, 2008.

---. *Women Writers of the Middle Ages: A Critical Study of Texts from Perpetua*. 1st ed., Cambridge University Press, 1985.

E-Reader | Beyond Clinical Dehumanisation towards the Other in Communi. https://www.taylorfrancis.com/reader/download/f13728cd-c8ba-4798-a6d4-9db025a686e5/book/pdf?context=ubx. Accessed 25 Mar. 2025.

E-Reader | The Virtual Liturgy and Ritual Artifacts in Medieval and Ea. https://www.taylorfrancis.com/reader/download/ebe1157a-cc42-4940-aec8-ed822b867fb4/book/pdf?context=ubx. Accessed 27 Mar. 2025.

Esser, Annette. *The Hildegard of Bingen Pilgrimage Book*. Liturgical Press, 2022.

Evans, C. P. *Hildegard of Bingen, Two Hagiographies: Vita Sancti Rupperti Confessoris and Vita Sancti Dysibodi Episcopi*. Bilingual edition, Peeters, 2010.

FAQ. http://www.hildegard-society.org/p/faq.html. Accessed 15 Mar. 2025.

Fassler, Margot E. *Cosmos, Liturgy, and the Arts in the Twelfth Century: Hildegard's Illuminated "Scivias."* University of Pennsylvania Press, 2022.

Ferracuti, Stefano, and Roberto Sacco. "Dissociative Trance Disorder: Clinical and Rorschach Findings in Ten Persons Reporting Demon Possession and Treated by Exorcism." *Journal of Personality Assessment*, vol. 66, no. 3, June 1996, p. 525. *EBSCOhost*, https://doi.org/10.1207/s15327752jpa6603_4.

Fictional Goal/Guiding Fiction/Fictional Finalism | AdlerPedia. https://www.adlerpedia.org/concepts/45. Accessed 8 Nov. 2024.

Field, Sean. "Review of Discerning Spirits: Divine and Demonic Possession in the Middle Ages." *Speculum*, vol. 80, no. 2, 2005, pp. 531–33.

Flanagan, Sabina. *Hildegard of Bingen: A Visionary Life*. 2nd ed., Routledge, 1998.

Forcén, Carlos Espí, and Fernando Espí Forcén. "Demonic Possessions and Mental Illness: Discussion of Selected Cases in Late Medieval Hagiographical Literature." *Early Science and Medicine*, vol. 19, no. 3, 2014, pp. 258–79.

Freeman, Charles. *Holy Bones, Holy Dust: How Relics Shaped the History of Medieval Europe*. Yale University Press, 2011. *ProQuest Ebook Central*, http://ebookcentral.proquest.com/lib/csbsju/detail.action?docID=3420906.

Fuhrkkotter, Adelgundis and Mary Palmquist. *The Life of the Holy Hildegard*. Edited by John Kulas, Complete Numbers Starting with 1, 1st edition, Liturgical Pr, 1995.

Gao, Mengyu, et al. "Dynamics of Mother-infant Parasympathetic Regulation during

Works Cited

Face-to-face Interaction: The Role of Maternal Emotion Dysregulation." *Psychophysiology*, vol. 60, no. 6, June 2023, pp. 1–18. *EBSCOhost*, https://doi.org/10.1111/psyp.14248.

Gender Guiding Lines and Role Models | AdlerPedia. https://www.adlerpedia.org/concepts/56. Accessed 6 Nov. 2024.

Gilman, Sander L. "Madness as Disability." *History of Psychiatry*, vol. 25, no. 4, Dec. 2014, pp. 441–49. *SAGE Journals*, https://doi.org/10.1177/0957154X14545846.

Hahn, Cynthia. "What Do Reliquaries Do for Relics?" *Numen*, vol. 57, no. 3/4, 2010, pp. 284–316.

Harteloh, Peter. "Hildegard of Bingen: Philosophical Life and Spirituality." *Religions*, vol. 15, no. 4, 4, Apr. 2024, p. 506. *www.mdpi.com*, https://doi.org/10.3390/rel15040506.

Haver, Mary Claire. *The New Menopause: Navigating Your Path Through Hormonal Change with Purpose, Power, and Facts*. Rodale Books, 2024.

Healing in Community. - EBSCO. https://research.ebsco.com/c/libxgu/viewer/html/tszolgph7b?route=details. Accessed 25 Mar. 2025.

Hearing Spiritual Voices. http://www.bloomsburycollections.com/collections/monograph. Accessed 25 Mar. 2025.

Henriksen, Mads Gram and Josef Parnas. "Mysticism and Schizophrenia: A Phenomenological Exploration of the Structure of Consciousness in the Schizophrenia Spectrum Disorders." *Consciousness and Cognition*, vol. 43, July 2016, pp. 75–88. *ScienceDirect*, https://doi.org/10.1016/j.concog.2016.05.010.

Heredity (Genetic Possibility)/Environment (Environmental Opportunity) | AdlerPedia. https://www.adlerpedia.org/concepts/112. Accessed 7 Nov. 2024.

Hildegard of Bingen. *The Book of Divine Works*. Translated by Nathaniel M. Campbell, The Catholic University of America Press, 2021.

——. *Hildegard of Bingen: On Natural Philosophy and Medicine*. Translated by Margret Berger, D. S. Brewer, 1999.

——. *Hildegard of Bingen: Scivias*. Translated by Mother Columba Hart and Jane Bishop, First Edition, Paulist Press, 1990.

——. *Hildegard von Bingen's Physica: The Complete English Translation of Her Classic Work on Health and Healing*. Translated by Priscilla Throop, First Edition, Healing Arts Press, 1998.

——. *The Book of the Rewards of Life: Liber Vitae Meritorum*. Translated by Bruce W. Hozeski, Oxford University Press, 1997.

——. *Hildegard of Bingen: Essential Writings and Chants of a Christian Mystic—Annotated & Explained*. Translated by Sheryl A. Kujawa-Holbrook, 1st ed., SkyLight Paths, 2016.

Hühne-Osterloh, G., and G. Grupe. "Causes of Infant Mortality in the Middle Ages Revealed by Chemical and Palaeopathological Analyses of Skeletal Remains." *Zeitschrift Für Morphologie Und Anthropologie*, vol. 77, no. 3, 1989, pp. 247–58.

Inquirer. "Doctor Diet, Doctor Quiet and Doctor Merryman." *Journal of the American Medical Association*, vol. XXIII, no. 19, Nov. 1894, pp. 732–732. https://doi.org/10.1001/jama.1894.02421240030012.

Works Cited

Jong, Mayke De. "Introduction." *In Samuel's Image*, Brill, 1996, pp. 1–15. *brill.com*, https://doi.org/10.1163/9789004246614_002.

Keirsey, David. *Please Understand Me II: Temperament, Character, Intelligence*. First Edition, Prometheus Nemesis Book Co, 1998.

Kelly, Timothy A. *Healing the Broken Mind*.

Kemp, Simon. "Mental Disorder and Mysticism in the Late Medieval World." *History of Psychology*, vol. 22, no. 2, May 2019, pp. 149–62. *EBSCOhost*, https://doi.org/10.1037/hop0000121.

Kinghorn, Warren. "Mental Disorder and Religious Experience: The Need for a Humble, Pragmatic Pluralism." *Philosophy, Psychiatry, & Psychology*, vol. 31, no. 3, 2024, pp. 215–17.

Kircanski, Katharina, et al. "Aberrant Parasympathetic Stress Responsivity in Pure and Co-Occurring Major Depressive Disorder and Generalized Anxiety Disorder." *Journal of Psychopathology and Behavioral Assessment*, vol. 38, no. 1, Mar. 2016, pp. 5–19. *Springer Link*, https://doi.org/10.1007/s10862-015-9493-y.

Kirsch, Irving. "The Placebo Effect Revisited: Lessons Learned to Date." *Complementary Therapies in Medicine*, vol. 21, no. 2, June 2013, pp. 102–04. *EBSCOhost*, https://doi.org/10.1016/j.ctim.2012.12.003.

Kroll, Jerome L. "Hildegard: Medieval Holism and 'Presentism'—: Or, Did Sigewiza Have Health Insurance?" *Philosophy, Psychiatry, & Psychology*, vol. 14, no. 4, 2007, pp. 369–72.

Lafferty, Sean. "Ad Sanctitatem Mortuorum: Tomb Raiders, Body Snatchers and Relic Hunters in Late Antiquity." *Early Medieval Europe*, vol. 22, no. 3, Aug. 2014, pp. 249–79. *EBSCOhost*, https://doi.org/10.1111/emed.12062.

Lee, Christina and Wendy J. Turner. *Trauma in Medieval Society*. BRILL, 2018. *ProQuest Ebook Central*, http://ebookcentral.proquest.com/lib/csbsju/detail.action?docID=5449676.

Lewis, Mary. "Children Aren't Starting Puberty Younger, Medieval Skeletons Reveal." *The Conversation*, 12 Feb. 2018, http://theconversation.com/children-arent-starting-puberty-younger-medieval-skeletons-reveal-91095.

Liu, Yu, et al. "Harmonious Healing: Advances in Music Therapy and Other Alternative Therapy for Depression and Beyond." *Brain Behavior and Immunity Integrative*, vol. 8, Dec. 2024, p. 100094. *ScienceDirect*, https://doi.org/10.1016/j.bbii.2024.100094.

Luethje, Kathy. *Healing with Art and Soul: Engaging One's Self through Art Modalities*. Cambridge Scholars Publishing, 2009. *ProQuest Ebook Central*, http://ebookcentral.proquest.com/lib/csbsju/detail.action?docID=1114407.

Macnaughton, Jane and Heather Yoeli. "'To More than I Can Be': A Phenomenological Meta-Ethnography of Singing Groups for People with Chronic Obstructive Pulmonary Disease." *Health*, vol. 25, no. 5, Sept. 2021, pp. 574–95. *SAGE Journals*, https://doi.org/10.1177/1363459320978520.

Maddocks, Fiona. *Hildegard of Bingen: The Woman of Her Age*. Main edition, Faber & Faber, 2013.

Works Cited

Maniacci, Michael, and Harold Mosak. *Primer of Adlerian Psychology*. 1st ed., Routledge, 1999.

Measuring Happiness in the Social Sciences: An Overview. https://doi.org/10.1177/1440783321991655. Accessed 14 Mar. 2025.

Million, Dian. *Therapeutic Nations: Healing in an Age of Indigenous Human Rights*. University of Arizona Press, 2013. *ProQuest Ebook Central*, http://ebookcentral.proquest.com/lib/csbsju/detail.action?docID=3411836.

Mitchem, Stephanie. *African American Folk Healing*. New York University Press, 2007. *ProQuest Ebook Central*, http://ebookcentral.proquest.com/lib/csbsju/detail.action?docID=865703.

Moerman, Daniel E., et al. "Anthropology of Symbolic Healing [and Comments and Reply]." *Current Anthropology*, vol. 20, no. 1, 1979, pp. 59–80.

Mogil, Jeffrey S. "Placebo Effect Involves Unexpected Brain Regions." *Nature*, vol. 632, no. 8027, Aug. 2024, pp. 990–91. *www.nature.com*, https://doi.org/10.1038/d41586-024-02373-x.

Mulder-Bakker, Anneke B. "Anchorites in the Low Countries." *Anchoritic Traditions of Medieval Europe*, edited by Liz Herbert McAvoy, Boydell & Brewer, 2010, pp. 22–42. *JSTOR*, https://www.jstor.org/stable/10.7722/j.ctt81hf3.8.

Nagoski, Amelia, and Emily Nagoski. *Burnout: The Secret to Unlocking the Stress Cycle*. Random House Publishing Group, 2020.

Nešić, Janko, et al. "The Therapeutic Role of the Monastic Environment for Individuals with ASC: The Case of Hildegard of Bingen and Her Lingua Ignota." *Eidos. A Journal for Philosophy of Culture*, vol. 8, no. 2, Aug. 2024, pp. 7–26. *doaj.org*, https://doi.org/10.14394/eidos.jpc.2024.0008.

"New Study Reveals Four Major Personality Types." *The Johns Hopkins News-Letter*, https://www.jhunewsletter.com/article/2018/10/new-study-reveals-four-major-personality-types. Accessed 15 Mar. 2025.

Newbauer, John F. "Everything Can Also Be Different: From Clinical Observation to Lifelong Motif." *Journal of Individual Psychology*, vol. 80, no. 1, Mar. 2024, pp. 3–14. *EBSCOhost*, https://doi.org/10.1353/jip.2024.a922701.

Newman, Barbara. *Sister of Wisdom: St. Hildegard's Theology of the Feminine*. First Edition, With a New Preface, Bibliography, and Discography, University of California Press, 1998.

———. *Voice of the Living Light: Hildegard of Bingen and Her World*. First Edition, University of California Press, 1998.

Nyashanu, Mathew, et al. "Evaluating the Benefits of Inclusive Community Singing towards Well-Being: Narratives of Diverse Community Members Attending an Inclusive Singing Group." *Journal of Public Mental Health*, vol. 20, no. 4, 2021, pp. 312–19. *ProQuest*, https://doi.org/10.1108/JPMH-05-2021-0061.

Papadimitriou, Anastasios. "The Evolution of the Age at Menarche from Prehistorical to Modern Times." *Journal of Pediatric and Adolescent Gynecology*, vol. 29, no. 6, Dec. 2016, pp. 527–30. *ScienceDirect*, https://doi.org/10.1016/j.jpag.2015.12.002.

Park, Soyoung Q., et al. "A Neural Link between Generosity and Happiness." *Nature*

Works Cited

Communications, vol. 8, no. 1, July 2017, p. 15964. *DOI.org (Crossref)*, https://doi.org/10.1038/ncomms15964. Accessed 14 Mar. 2025.

Peretz, Isabelle, and Dominique T. Vuvan. "Prevalence of Congenital Amusia." *European Journal of Human Genetics*, vol. 25, no. 5, May 2017, pp. 625–30. *PubMed Central*, https://doi.org/10.1038/ejhg.2017.15.

Perry, Bruce D. and Oprah Winfrey. *What Happened to You?: Conversations on Trauma, Resilience, and Healing*. 1st ed., Flatiron Books: An Oprah Book, 2021.

Porter, Chris L., et al. "Development of Mother-Infant Co-Regulation: The Role of Infant Vagal Tone and Temperament at 6, 9, and 12 Months of Age." *Infant Behavior and Development*, vol. 67, May 2022, p. 101708. *ScienceDirect*, https://doi.org/10.1016/j.infbeh.2022.101708.

Radden, Jennifer H. *The Nature of Melancholy: From Aristotle to Kristeva*. Oxford University Press, Incorporated, 2000. *ProQuest Ebook Central*, http://ebookcentral.proquest.com/lib/csbsju/detail.action?docID=431206.

Radden, Jennifer H. "Sigewiza's Cure." *Philosophy, Psychiatry, & Psychology*, vol. 14, no. 4, 2007, pp. 373–76.

Ranft, Patricia. "Ruminations on Hildegard of Bingen (1098-1179) and Autism." *Journal of Medical Biography*, vol. 22, no. 2, May 2014, pp. 107–15. *PubMed*, https://doi.org/10.1177/0967772013479283.

Rath, Philippa, et al. *Hildegard of Bingen: Historical Sites*. 3rd ed., Schnell & Steiner, 2014.

Reichelt, Lauren. "Healing in Community." *Tikkun*, vol. 25, no. 2, Apr. 2010, pp. 19–22. *DOI.org (Crossref)*, https://doi.org/10.1215/08879982-2010-2007.

Rite Meaning - Google Search. Accessed 21 Mar. 2025.

Ritual Meaning - Google Search. Accessed 21 Mar. 2025.

"Rituals and Rites of Passage in Society | Overview & Examples - Lesson." *Study.Com*, https://study.com/academy/lesson/rituals-rites-of-passage-in-society.html. Accessed 21 Mar. 2025.

Routine Meaning - Google Search. Accessed 21 Mar. 2025.

Rowe, Nick, et al. *Applied Practice: Evidence and Impact in Theatre, Music and Art*. Bloomsbury Publishing Plc, 2017. *ProQuest Ebook Central*, http://ebookcentral.proquest.com/lib/csbsju/detail.action?docID=4913729.

Rozgonjuk, Dmitri, et al. "The Affective Neuroscience Personality Scales: Linking the Adjective and Statement-Based Inventories with the Big Five Inventory in English and German-Speaking Samples." *Personality Neuroscience*, vol. 4, Jan. 2021, p. e7. *Cambridge University Press*, https://doi.org/10.1017/pen.2021.6.

Ruys, Juanita Feros. "Demonic Possession and Lived Religion in Later Medieval Europe." *Church History*, vol. 90, no. 4, Dec. 2021, pp. 940–42. *EBSCOhost*, https://doi.org/10.1017/s0009640722000270.

The Sacred Body: Materializing the Divine through Human Remains in Antiquity. Vol. 1, Oxbow Books, 2021. *JSTOR*, https://doi.org/10.2307/j.ctv13nb8wc.

Schmid, Regina Franziska, et al. "Individual Differences in Parasympathetic Nervous System Reactivity in Response to Everyday Stress Are Associated with

Works Cited

Momentary Emotional Exhaustion." *Scientific Reports*, vol. 14, no. 1, Nov. 2024, p. 26662. *www.nature.com*, https://doi.org/10.1038/s41598-024-74873-9.

Schultz, James A. "Medieval Adolescence: The Claims of History and the Silence of German Narrative." *Speculum*, vol. 66, no. 3, 1991, pp. 519–39. *JSTOR*, https://doi.org/10.2307/2864225.

"*Scivias*"-Code: Panel 4: The Universe – BENEDICAT RESULT ST. HILDEGARD. https://abtei-st-hildegard.de/%e2%80%9cscivias%e2%80%9d-kodex-tafel-4-das-weltall/. Accessed 26 Mar. 2025.

"*Scivias*"-Code: Panel 9: The Choirs of the Angels – BENEDIC SECTORS ST. HILDEGARD. https://abtei-st-hildegard.de/%e2%80%9cscivias%e2%80%9d-kodex-tafel-9-die-chore-der-engel/. Accessed 26 Mar. 2025.

Seftel, Laura. *Grief Unseen: Healing Pregnancy Loss Through the Arts*. Jessica Kingsley Publishers, 2006. *ProQuest Ebook Central*, http://ebookcentral.proquest.com/lib/csbsju/detail.action?docID=290894.

Shilton, Dor, et al. "Group Singing Is Globally Dominant and Associated with Social Context." *Royal Society Open Science*, vol. 10, no. 9, p. 230562. *PubMed Central*, https://doi.org/10.1098/rsos.230562.

Shin, In-Cheol. "The Purpose of the Theological Patterns in Jesus' Healing Stories in the Gospel of Matthew." *HTS Theological Studies*, vol. 79, no. 2, Dec. 2023, pp. 1–9. *EBSCOhost*, https://doi.org/10.4102/hts.v79i2.8893.

Signori, Gabriela. "Anchorites in German-Speaking Regions." *Anchoritic Traditions of Medieval Europe*, edited by Liz Herbert McAvoy, Boydell & Brewer, 2010, pp. 43–61. *JSTOR*, https://www.jstor.org/stable/10.7722/j.ctt81hf3.9.

Silvas, Anna. *Jutta and Hildegard: The Biographical Sources*. 1st ed., Penn State University Press, 1999.

St. Hildegard on Gemstones – Unam Sanctam Catholicam. https://unamsanctamcatholicam.com/2022/04/25/st-hildegard-on-gemstones/. Accessed 20 Mar. 2025.

Sweet, Victoria. *God's Hotel: A Doctor, a Hospital, and a Pilgrimage to the Heart of Medicine*. Reprint edition, Riverhead Books, 2013.

———. *Rooted in the Earth, Rooted in the Sky*. 1st ed., Routledge, 2006.

Tapping the Healing Rhythms of the Vagal Nerve | Psychology Today. https://www.psychologytoday.com/us/blog/arts-and-health/202004/tapping-the-healing-rhythms-of-the-vagal-nerve. Accessed 27 Mar. 2025.

The Therapeutic Role of the Monastic Environment for Individuals with ASC: The Case of Hildegard of Bingen and Her Lingua Ignota – Eidos. A Journal for Philosophy of Culture. https://eidos.uw.edu.pl/the-therapeutic-role-of-the-monastic-environment-for-individuals-with-asc-the-case-of-hildegard-of-bingen-and-her-lingua-ignota/. Accessed 25 Mar. 2025.

———. https://eidos.uw.edu.pl/the-therapeutic-role-of-the-monastic-environment-for-individuals-with-asc-the-case-of-hildegard-of-bingen-and-her-lingua-ignota/. Accessed 27 Mar. 2025.

Thram, Diane. "Understanding Music's Therapeutic Efficacy: Implications for Music Education." *The Journal for Transdisciplinary Research in Southern Africa*, vol. 10, no. 2, Nov. 2014, p. 13.

Works Cited

Throop, Priscilla. *Causes and Cures of Hildegard of Bingen*. 2nd ed., MedievalMS, 2012.

Trethowan, W. H., et al. "Exorcism: A Psychiatric Viewpoint [with Comment]." *Journal of Medical Ethics*, vol. 2, no. 3, 1976, pp. 127–37.

Trevett, Christine. "Asperger's Syndrome and the Holy Fool: The Case of Brother Juniper." *Journal of Religion, Disability & Health*, vol. 13, no. 2, Dec. 2009, pp. 129–50. *EBSCOhost*, https://doi.org/10.1080/15228960802581537.

Utah State University. *Does Giving Make You Happier? Or Do Happier People Give? - Discovery Fall 2017 - Science*. https://www.usu.edu/science/discovery/fall-2017/does-giving-make-you-happy. Accessed 14 Mar. 2025.

van der Kolk, Bessel. *The Body Keeps the Score: Brain, Mind, and Body in the Healing of Trauma*. Reprint edition, Penguin Books, 2015.

Verschuere, Bruno, et al. "The Ease of Lying." *Consciousness and Cognition*, vol. 20, no. 3, Sept. 2011, pp. 908–11. *ScienceDirect*, https://doi.org/10.1016/j.concog.2010.10.023.

Vincent, Nicholas. "Discerning Spirits: Divine and Demonic Possession in the Middle Ages." *The Journal of Ecclesiastical History*, vol. 59, no. 1, Dec. 2008, pp. 118–19. *EBSCOhost*, https://doi.org/10.1017/S0022046907002734.

von Davier, Matthias, et al. "Factorial Versus Typological Models: A Comparison of Methods for Personality Data." *Measurement*, vol. 10, no. 4, Oct. 2012, pp. 185–208. *EBSCOhost*, https://doi.org/10.1080/15366367.2012.732798.

Why We Need to Talk about Losing a Baby. https://www.who.int/news-room/spotlight/why-we-need-to-talk-about-losing-a-baby. Accessed 5 Nov. 2024.

Wiśniewski, Robert. *The Beginnings of the Cult of Relics*. Oxford University Press, Incorporated, 2019. *ProQuest Ebook Central*, http://ebookcentral.proquest.com/lib/csbsju/detail.action?docID=5606643.

Wu, Dingcheng, et al. "Neural Correlates of Evaluations of Lying and Truth-Telling in Different Social Contexts." *Brain Research*, vol. 1389, May 2011, pp. 115–24. *ScienceDirect*, https://doi.org/10.1016/j.brainres.2011.02.084.

Additional Resources

ALFRED ADLER

Alfred Adler's Works

Adler, Alfred. *The Practice and Theory of Individual Psychology (1925)*. Martino Fine Books, 2011.
____. *Understanding Human Nature (1927)*. Martino Fine Books, 2010.
____. *The Science of Living (1929)*. McAllister Editions, 2015.
____. *What Life Should Mean To You (1932)*. Martino Fine Books, 1990.
____. *The Collected Clinical Works of Alfred Adler, Volumes 1-12*. Alfred Adler Institute, 2002.
Drescher, Karen. *Adler Speaks: The Lectures of Alfred Adler*. iUniverse, 2004.

General Resources

Ansbacher, Heinz L., and Rowena R. Ansbacher, editors. *The Individual Psychology of Alfred Adler: A Systematic Presentation in Selections from His Writings*. Harper Perennial, 1964.
Carlson, Jon, et al. *Adlerian Therapy: Theory and Practice*. Amer Psychological Assn, 2006.
Carlson, Jon, and Michael P. Maniacci, editors. *Alfred Adler Revisited*. Routledge, 2012.
Dreikurs, Sadie E., et al. *Cows Can Be Purple*. Edited by Nancy Catlin Ph.D. and James Croake Ph.D., Adler School of Professional Psychology, 1986.
Ferguson, Eva Dreikurs. *Adlerian Theory: An Introduction*. CreateSpace, 2009.
Maniacci, Michael, and Harold Mosak. *Primer of Adlerian Psychology*. 1st ed., Routledge, 1999.
Powers, Robert L., and Jane Griffith. *The Key to Psychotherapy: Understanding the Self-Created Individual*. Adlerian Psychology Associates, Ltd., 2012.

Child Guidance

Dreikurs, Rudolf, and Vicki Stolz. *Children: The Challenge: The Classic Work on Improving Parent-Child Relations--Intelligent, Humane & Eminently Practical*. Plume, 1990.
Dreikurs, Rudolf, et al. *Discipline Without Tears: How to Reduce Conflict and Establish Cooperation in the Classroom*. Wiley, 2004.

Additional Resources

Glenn, H. Stephen, and Jane Nelsen. *Raising Self-Reliant Children in a Self-Indulgent World: Seven Building Blocks for Developing Capable Young People*. Harmony, 2010.

Nelsen, Jane. *Positive Discipline: The Classic Guide to Helping Children Develop Self-Discipline, Responsibility, Cooperation, and Problem-Solving Skills*. Ballantine Books, 2011.

Nelsen, Jane, et al. *Positive Discipline: The First Three Years, Revised and Updated Edition: From Infant to Toddler--Laying the Foundation for Raising a Capable, Confident*. Harmony, 2015.

HILDEGARD OF BINGEN

English Translations of Hildegard's Works

Compilations

Butcher, Carmen Acevedo. *Hildegard of Bingen, Doctor of the Church: A Spiritual Reader*. Paraclete Press, 2013.

———. *Incandescence: 365 Readings with Women Mystics*. Brewster: Paraclete Press, 2005.

Hildegard of Bingen. *Hildegard of Bingen: Selected Writings*. Edited by Mark Atherton. London: Penguin Books, 2001.

———. *Prayers of Holy Hildegard*. Edited by Walburga Storch. Collegeville: The Liturgical Press, 1997.

———. *Hildegard of Bingen: Essential Writings and Chants of a Christian Mystic—Annotated & Explained*. Translated by Sheryl A. Kujawa-Holbrook, 1st ed., SkyLight Paths, 2016.

Letters

Hildegard of Bingen. *The Letters of Hildegard of Bingen*. Edited by Joseph L. Baird and Radd K. Ehrman. Vol. 1. 3 vols. New York: Oxford University Press, 1994.

———. *The Letters of Hildegard of Bingen*. Edited by Joseph L. Baird and Radd K. Ehrman. Vol. 2. 3 vols. New York: Oxford University Press, 1998.

———. *The Letters of Hildegard of Bingen*. Edited by Joseph L. Baird and Radd K. Ehrman. Vol. 3. 3 vols. Oxford: Oxford University Press, 2004.

———. *The Personal Correspondence of Hildegard of Bingen*. Edited by Joseph L. Baird. Oxford: Oxford University Press, 2006.

Additional Resources

Medicine

Hildegard of Bingen. *Hildegard of Bingen: On Natural Philosophy and Medicine.* Translated by Margret Berger, D. S. Brewer, 1999.

___. *Hildegard von Bingen's Physica: The Complete English Translation of Her Classic Work on Health and Healing.* Translated by Priscilla Throop, 1st Ed., Healing Arts Press, 1998.

___. *Causes and Cures.* Translated by Priscilla Throop, Charlotte, Vermont: Medieval MS, 2006.

Music

Hildegard of Bingen. *Symphonia: A Critical Edition of the Symphonia armonie celestium revelationum [Symphony of the Harmony of Celestial Revelations].* Edited by Barbara Newman. Ithaca: Cornell University Press, 1988.

Sermons

Hildegard of Bingen. *Hildegard of Bingen: Homilies on the Gospels.* Edited by Beverly Mayne Kienzle. Collegeville: Liturgical Press, 2011.

Kienzle, Beverly Mayne. *Hildegard of Bingen Gospel Interpreter.* Lanham: Lexington Books/Fortress Academic, 2020.

Visions

Hildegard of Bingen. *The Book of Divine Works.* Translated by Nathaniel M. Campbell, The Catholic University of America Press, 2021.

___. *Hildegard of Bingen: Scivias.* Translated by Mother Columba Hart and Jane Bishop, 1st ed., Paulist Press, 1990.

___. *The Book of the Rewards of Life: Liber Vitae Meritorum.* Translated by Bruce W. Hozeski. Oxford University Press, 1997.

General Resources

Benedict of Nursia. *The Rule of Saint Benedict: A Contemporary Paraphrase.* Edited by Jonathan Wilson-Hartgrove, Paraclete Press, 2012.

Craine, Renate. *Hildegard: Prophet of the Cosmic Christ.* New York: The Crossroad Publishing Company, 1997.

Dronke, Peter. *Women Writers of the Middle Ages: A Critical Study of Texts from Perpetua.* 1st ed., Cambridge University Press, 1985.

Esser, Annette. *The Hildegard of Bingen Pilgrimage Book.* Liturgical Press, 2022.

___. *Hildegard Speaks.* Crazy Wisdom Publishing, 2022.

Evans, C. P. *Hildegard of Bingen, Two Hagiographies: Vita Sancti Rupperti Confessoris and Vita Sancti Dysibodi Episcopi.* Bilingual edition, Peeters, 2010.

Flanagan, Sabina. *Hildegard of Bingen: A Visionary Life.* 2nd ed., Routledge, 1998.

Fox, Matthew. *Hildegard of Bingen: A Saint for Our Times.* Namaste Publishing, 2012.

Fuhrkkotter, Adelgundis and Mary Palmquist. *The Life of the Holy Hildegard.* Edited by John Kulas, Complete Numbers Starting with 1, 1st ed., Liturgical Press, 1995.

Additional Resources

Gottfried and Theoderic. *The Life of the Holy Hildegard*. Edited by Mary Palmquist and John Kulas. Collegeville: The Order of St. Benedict Incorporated, 1995.

King-Lenzmeier, Anne H. *Hildegard of Bingen: An Integrated Vision*. Collegeville: Liturgical Press, 2001.

Maddocks, Fiona. *Hildegard of Bingen: The Woman of Her Age*. Main edition, Faber & Faber, 2013.

Newman, Barbara. *Sister of Wisdom: St. Hildegard's Theology of the Feminine*. 1st ed., With a New Preface, Bibliography, and Discography, University of California Press, 1998.

——. *Voice of the Living Light: Hildegard of Bingen and Her World*. 1st ed., University of California Press, 1998.

Rath, Philippa, et al. *Hildegard of Bingen: Historical Sites*. 3rd ed., Schnell & Steiner, 2014.

Sterringer, Shanon. 2019. *30-Day Journey with St. Hildegard of Bingen*. Minneapolis: Fortress Press.

——. *Forbidden Grace: Hildegard of Bingen and a Modern Women's Call to the Catholic Priesthood*. Independently published, 2023.

Silvas, Anna. *Jutta and Hildegard: The Biographical Sources*. 1st ed., Penn State University Press, 1999.

Medical/Mental Health

Cannon, Sue. *Hildegard of Bingen Holistic Health Visionary: Twelfth-Century Medical Theories with Modern-Day Appeal*. Independently published, 2023.

Clendenen, Avis. *Experiencing Hildegard: Jungian Perspectives*. Wilmette: Chiron Publications, 2012.

Hertzka, Gottfried and Wighard Strehlow. *Hildegard of Bingen's Medicine*. Rochester, Vermont: Bear & Company, 1988.

Schipperges, Heinrich. *Hildegard of Bingen: Healing and the Nature of the Cosmos*. Translated by John A. Broadwin. Princeton, NJ: Markus Wiener Publishers, 1997.

Strehlow, Wighard. *Hildegard of Bingen: Spiritual Remedies*. Rochester, Vermont: Healing Arts Press, 2002.

Sweet, Victoria. *God's Hotel: A Doctor, a Hospital, and a Pilgrimage to the Heart of Medicine*. Reprint edition, Riverhead Books, 2013.

——. *Rooted in the Earth, Rooted in the Sky*. 1st ed., Routledge, 2006.

Music, Drama, and Art

Boyce-Tillman, June. *The Creative Spirit: Harmonious Living with Hildegard of Bingen*. Norwich: Canterbury Press, 2000.

Davidson, Audrey Ekdahl. *The Ordo Virtutum of Hildegard of Bingen: Critical Studies*. Medieval Institute Publications, 1992.

Dronke, Peter, editor. *Nine Medieval Latin Plays*. Cambridge University Press, 2008.

Additional Resources

Fassler, Margot E. *Cosmos, Liturgy, and the Arts in the Twelfth Century: Hildegard's Illuminated "Scivias."* University of Pennsylvania Press, 2022.

Hutchinson, Gloria. *A Retreat with Gerard Manley Hopkins and Hildegard of Bingen: Turning Pain into Power.* Cincinnati: St. Anthony Messenger Press, 1995.

Salvadori, Sara. *Hildegard von Bingen: A Journey Into the Images.* Milano: Skira Editori, 2019.

____. *Hildegard von Bingen: In the Heart of God.* Milano: Skira Editori, 2021.

Fiction

Keating, Colleen. *Hildegard of Bingen: A Poetic Journey.* Port Adelaide: Ginninderra Press, 2019.

O'Hanneson, Joan. *Scarlet Music: A Life of Hildegard von Bingen.* Crossroad, 1998.

Sharratt, Mary. *Illuminations: A Novel of Hildegard von Bingen.* Mariner Books, 2012.

Acknowledgments

This work could never have come about without many hands and hearts building it with me. As Hildegard and Adler wisely knew, community heals.

Without Keely, I never would have found the guidebook or had places to stay. Her gift for languages, abiding friendship, and wisdom in knowing I needed a pilgrimage is something for which I will forever be grateful.

All those who donated to my "When the Church Hurts, Friends Heal" GoFundMe and those who prayed, raged, and cared for me during that liminal time. I carry your kindness and support in my heart forever.

The Rt. Rev. Melissa Skelton, Bishop Provisional during the time of my pilgrimage: Your immediate support of the pilgrimage and ministry of presence meant so much.

Dr. Annette Esser, for the idea and invitation of doing the presentation that led to this book. Your friendship and creativity are a gift. I look forward to further collaboration!

Dr. Victoria Sweet, your kindness and encouragement meant the world to me. Slow medicine and Hildegard forever.

Rev. Dr. Angela Yarber, thank you for wanting this book and for making Tehom Center Publishing a womb of God's love in order to birth the best writing.

Sister Phillipa Rath at the Abtei St. Hildegard, Rüdesheim am Rhein: Vielen Dank for your patience with my Google translated German and getting the illuminated images to me for this book.

The Writers' Colony at Dairy Hollow: Wow. Just wow. Jess,

Jeanne, Helke, and especially Crescent Dragonwagon (for pinch hitting our dinners). Shout out to Harold's Diner – ya'll keep dancing you hear?

My Minnesota hospitality crew: Gretchen (for everything always—there are not enough words), Adam (the loyalist of friends from moving boxes of rocks to driving me around), Sonja (for Costco and taking time for me), Diana (TCP writing partner and encouragement), and Carol (for hospitality to this stranger).

The Collegeville Institute: Carla, Nancy, the St. John's University Library staff, and the incredible Residents (you know who you are!) who came alongside me to help birth this. I owe the title of this book to you.

Sacred Waters Center for Restoration and Retreat: Dan, Lois, and Candy gave me space to finish my draft. Hillside Cottage will forever hold a special place in my heart.

Church of the Nativity, Sandy Cove, Nova Scotia: Thank you to this fine community for inviting me to be with them while I finished the second draft and first round of edits holed up in their Rectory—especially John, Alana, and Evie. They have the best summer garden parties!

My Hildegard Reading/Editing Team: Rev. Dr. Shanon Sterringer (Hildegard expert and priest extraordinaire), Rev. LeeAnn Pomrenke (simply the best editor in the universe and literary adventure partner), Kathleen Wiley (Jungian analyst and soul sister), Rev. Diana McLean (divine copy editor), Kate Walker (fellow Celtic Queen), and Molly O'Dell (splendid poet and inspired physician). Thank you for the hours you put into making this the best book possible. Some of the best ideas came from them.

Kester Limner, you are a DREAM illustrator to collaborate with! You captured the spirit of the project from the first moment we talked about it and brought the whole thing to life. Thank you is not remotely enough to express my appreciation of you and your artistry. You are magic!

To Shelley (the Diana to my Anne), Darlyn (my anamchara), Mom, Jason (all the encouraging quotes each writing day while at

Collegeville), and multitudes of friends, family, colleagues, and Hildegard and Adler admirers who cheered me on in this endeavor. Thank you for celebrating my commitment to this work and dosing me with glitter (real and in spirit) along the way!

To Henry, mo chroí—your superb editing, encouragement, and devotion to me doing this work says everything. Thank you for mitigating Cooper's unflagging energy for rope tug and playing Jolly Ball so that I could work in my Goddess Dwelling and around the world in peace. I could not have created this without you.

www.ingramcontent.com/pod-product-compliance
Lightning Source LLC
LaVergne TN
LVHW012039070526
838202LV00056B/5546